From Awareness *to Action*

Strategies to Stop Sexual Harassment
in the Workplace

Compiled and edited by
Linda Geller-Schwartz
for the Women's Bureau
Human Resources Development Canada

Également disponible en français sous le titre :
Comprendre pour agir, Stratégies d'élimination du harcèlement sexuel en milieu de travail

Published by authority of the Government of Canada

Additional copies may be obtained from:

> Publications Distribution Centre
> Human Resources Development Canada
> Ottawa, Ontario
> K1A 0J2
> Telephone: (819) 994-0543

© Minister of Supply and Services Canada
Catalogue No. L38-49/1993 E
ISBN 0-662-20851-X

Printed in Canada

1994 International Year of the Family
Année internationale de la famille

CONTENTS

iii

Section I

Introduction

Introduction

Sexual harassment is not innocent fun. It can devastate the life and livelihood of the victim, damage the career of the harasser and poison the workplace environment. The emotional and financial costs to everyone in the workplace can be enormous.

The Problem

There is a widespread misconception that only the most blatant form of sexual harassment amounting to criminal sexual assault is illegal in Canada. Anything less than sexual assault is too often regarded as mere "flirtation" or just "kidding around" rather than behaviour which is illegal and wrong.

Sexual harassment has always been defined more broadly in human rights legislation and accompanying policy statements. Recent court rulings have extended its scope further. In a 1989 decision, the Supreme Court of Canada defined sexual harassment as "...unwelcome conduct of a sexual nature that detrimentally affects the work environment or leads to adverse job-related consequences for the victims of the harassment." Sexual harassment in the workplace, as defined in these broad terms, is illegal in all provinces and territories in Canada, including those establishments that come under federal jurisdiction.

Yet studies of the problem in Canada and the United States show consistently that sexual harassment, although illegal, remains a serious and pervasive problem. From construction sites to professional offices, from universities to assembly lines, from restaurants to hospitals, the victims of sexual harassment dread entering the workplace and having to face once again the perpetrators of that harassment. They are subjected to distasteful jokes and lewd comments, pornographic pictures displayed on the workplace walls, intimidation, unwelcome physical contact and thinly veiled threats to their career prospects if they refuse to comply with sexual demands. The unfortunate victims are often placed in a grim dilemma. They fear the disbelief and ostracism they may face if they dare to complain but are unable to tolerate the endless harassment that renders their lives miserable.

Commitment to Change

Despite this grim view of the workplace, there may be grounds for optimism that the situation is beginning to change. A decade ago it would not have been possible to assemble a collection of essays by business and union leaders about sexual harassment. When Constance Backhouse and Leah Cohen were researching their pioneer study on sexual harassment in Canada in the late 1970s, they found that very few employers, personnel officers or union officials either understood the nature of sexual harassment or were prepared to acknowledge its seriousness and proportions. For many, sexual harassment was more of a joke than a problem.

By contrast, 15 years later, this volume demonstrates the dramatic change in consciousness about this issue. In the essays that follow, some of the largest employers in Canada, as well as labour organizations representing most unionized workers in this country, openly identify sexual harassment as a serious problem and declare their active commitment to eradicating it from the workplace.

The essays in this volume examine sexual harassment as a legal issue, a business issue and a social issue. They look at the strategies being adopted by employers and unions to deal with sexual harassment in a variety of workplaces. Together they provide an overview of the progress that has been made in addressing what is increasingly accepted as a serious issue.

None of the contributors to the volume believes that this is an easy task or that they are close to attaining their goal of "zero tolerance" for sexual harassment. However, each is convinced that a determined, proactive effort must be made to tackle the issue.

Tackling the Hard Questions

All the contributors to this volume share a resolve to deal with the problem of sexual harassment in the workplace. Yet each organization finds itself facing a somewhat different set of problems. For some, simply getting the issue of sexual harassment recognized as a real problem is a major first hurdle. Others have managed to develop policies, but communicating them to a very large, diverse, scattered work force presents a signficant challenge. Still others are at the stage of refining and revising policies that have been in place for some time in order to reflect a new understanding of how sexual harassment affects their work force or members.

The commitment of all partners in the workplace to grapple with the issues is heartening. The essays also demonstrate that employers and unions are prepared to examine and act upon some of the especially thorny problems that arise when there is a serious attempt to eliminate sexual harassment in the workplace.

For example, employers under federal jurisdiction are required by the *Canada Labour Code* to have a policy on sexual harassment which is posted in the workplace. Employers are beginning to recognize, however, that if they want to stop sexual harassment in the workplace, they must go beyond their legal obligations to make sure, by whatever means necessary, that everyone in the workplace is fully aware of the nature, meaning and consequences of such behaviour. They are spending time and money on innovative training programs and extensive information campaigns.

Employers are also looking closely at issues of accountability and responsibility. Legally, employers are responsible for maintaining a workplace free of harassment. Employers recognize, however, that in order to meet their responsibilities, everyone in the workplace, including senior management, middle management, individual supervisors and employees, must share a commitment to ending sexual harassment. So instead of simply leaving sexual harassment problems to be dealt with by human resource personnel, employers are looking for ways to instill a sense of accountability for workplace behaviour in all their employees.

Unions are also struggling with some complex issues. Co-worker harassment has always been a difficult problem for unions because of their obligation to support all their members. The essays in this volume demonstrate that many unions have done considerable work on this problem and are developing some creative and useful procedures that protect the legal rights of the victim and, at the same time, allow the union to fulfil its legal obligations to the alleged harasser who is also a union member.

The unions have been in the forefront in training their members and educating their officials about sexual harassment in order to try to stop harassment before it occurs. While recognizing that the employer has the primary legal responsibility to maintain a harassment-free workplace, unions acknowledge that, if their early intervention can eliminate complaints and grievances, everyone in the workplace will benefit. Thus unions are exploring the various informal mechanisms for handling complaints as well as developing educational programs that will ensure that all members recognize sexual harassment and understand its ramifications and consequences.

Accountability is also an issue for unions. Some unions have taken steps to ensure that all complaints are reported to senior union officials and then acted upon promptly at the local level. Some unions have also established a number of alternative channels within the union for filing complaints. These serve two purposes: the victim is ensured of getting a full and fair hearing and the leadership at all levels in the union can be held accountable for correcting problems of sexual harassment.

There has clearly been a significant change in the willingness of both unions and employers to accept a more interventionist role in addressing the problem of sexual harassment in the workplace.

Yet as important as this change has been, perhaps even more consequential has been the deepening understanding of the nature and causes of sexual harassment.

Understanding Sexual Harassment

It is evident from the essays that sexual harassment is no longer understood as "flirtation gone wrong" or a problem of unreciprocated attraction. Sexual harassment is about power and, more specifically, about the subordinate position of women in the workplace. Everyone acknowledges that in the vast majority of cases of sexual harassment, a woman is the victim and a man is the perpetrator. This pattern is not coincidental: it is both a manifestation and a result of women's unequal status in the workplace.

This understanding is gradually beginning to filter into the workplace. Employers are now recognizing that a program to combat sexual harassment is a legitimate part of an employment equity plan. Unions are teaching their members that pin-ups and other sexual material that many women find degrading seriously undermine efforts to foster a workplace based on equality and mutual respect between men and women.

It is beginning to be understood that perhaps the core of the problem is not sexual harassment but "gender harassment." Although the harassment may not be specifically "sexual" in nature, it is harassment directed at a woman specifically because she is a woman. In either case, the recipe for eliminating sexual harassment needs to be heavily weighted toward changing attitudes. There is a growing awareness among employers and unions that this is essential.

The Future Agenda

Optimism about change needs to be tempered with realism. While many unions and employers have travelled far along the road of understanding in the past decade, there is still a long way for everyone to go.

To what extent does the most senior management in corporations understand the significance of sexual harassment and have a commitment to eliminating it? As one contributor suggests, sexual harassment used to be considered a personal problem and now it has become a personnel problem. But when will it be generally considered a high-priority corporate problem?

Sexual harassment occurs in small businesses just as it does in large corporations. In most small businesses workers are less likely to have the protection and help of unions, so the victim of sexual harassment may be even more isolated. It is important for small businesses to recognize that they cannot ignore sexual harassment that occurs in their workplaces. Although their employees may be few in number, the human and financial costs of sexual harassment to the workers and the business as a whole can be staggering.

Some groups of women are among the most vulnerable workers in Canada: immigrant and visible minority women, native women and women with disabilities. These women frequently find themselves in the lowest paying, lowest status, least secure jobs. There is also some evidence that they may be more likely to be subjected to sexual harassment. In some notable cases, individuals were victims of both racial discrimination and sexual harassment. Women in these groups are in a doubly disadvantaged position in the workplace and, because of their economic vulnerability, are least able to risk fighting the harassment. Yet many have shown immense courage in fighting for their rights and their dignity. We all must become more aware of the special problems of harassment faced by these women and take steps to end the problem of double discrimination in the workplace.

In general, most recent efforts have focused on developing policies to discourage harassment and laying out the penalties for the harasser. There has been little focus on support for the victims. As one contributor points out, the nub of the problem is not the lone harasser but the silent complicity of everyone else in the workplace. The lack of support and the isolation in the workplace are perhaps the hardest part of the victim's ordeal. Unions and employers can play an important role in providing support for the victim. External support groups can also do much to sustain victims and help them fight the harassment. In most communities, however, victims of harassment have nowhere to turn for support.

We need to explore new legal tools for fighting sexual harassment and for getting compensation for victims. Sexual harassment is beginning to be recognized as an occupational health and safety issue. A recent important case has established that victims of sexual harassment can claim worker's compensation for the effects of racial and sexual harassment. In the United States, there are other legal routes to ensure that victims are properly compensated for the distress and injury they have suffered. Some of these avenues, which are discussed in this volume of essays, might be tried in Canada.

Finally, we also need to encourage the use of innovative, informal mechanisms to resolve complaints within the workplace. Most victims are primarily interested in getting the harasser to stop the harassment and to ensure that no one else is harassed. In some circumstances, mediation may be a suitable means to achieve the desired result but, as one of the contributors points out, there is room for other flexible, informal resolution mechanisms that will make the harasser fully comprehend the gravity of his conduct.

These are only some of the issues that need to be addressed. As our understanding of sexual harassment, its causes and consequences deepens, policies will have to be rewritten and new and better ways of communicating them will have to be found. This volume of essays gives reason for hope that many employers and unions, separately and as partners, are committed to eradicating sexual harassment from their workplaces. They know it will not be easy to do so, but they also know that a workplace built on mutual respect and equality is in their common interest.

Linda Geller-Schwartz

Section II

The Pervasiveness of the Problem:
From Courtrooms to Classrooms
to Construction Sites

Harassment: A Grassroots Perspective

Kate Braid

Kate Braid has been the Director of the Labour Program at Simon Fraser University since 1991. She also worked as a journeycarpenter for 15 years and has long been active on issues relating to women in trades and technology.

When a tradeswoman sets out to talk about sexual harassment, or even a day on the job, there is a distinct quickening of the pulse. As tradeswomen, we talk about this - the feeling that people seem to want to hear the graphic details at their worst, and that if we do not talk about these, we are not dealing with what is really going on.

There *are* horror stories. But these do not tell the whole story. After 15 years as a carpenter, I think that most analysts and commentators on the subject of harassment are biased by the fact of coming from a white-collar background that does not understand blue-collar work.

I am not saying that women in trades do not at times suffer severe harassment. We do, as do women in every career and every walk of life, and our goal in every workplace is to end it.

But I think that the harassment of tradeswomen must be seen in light of the culture and traditions of blue collar work, particularly the tradition of harassment in general and of harassment of apprentices and rookies in particular. But first, some background.

Sexual and Gender Harassment

My experience is that, in the 1970s, most tradesmen were convinced that a woman in their trade would fail and were impatient for her to get it over with. By the 1990s, instead of the attitude being one of "hurry up and fail," it is more often one of standing back to see what you can do. Fair enough. Harassment never ended, of course; it just changed.

Sexual harassment is sexually focused. It is the guy who runs up close behind you on the ladder and pushes his nose into your crotch. It is the foreman on a camp job who waits until you are asleep to try and crawl into your bed. It is the guy who flicks his tongue in and out suggestively when you walk by. These guys were typical of harassers in the late '70s and early '80s, when women were first moving onto construction sites and industrial workplaces in general. Even then, they were a minority, but a vicious one.

But something happened in the 1980s. Harassment became sophisticated and went underground. Those guys discovered gender harassment. When a friend of mine was an apprentice machinist, it was typical that her foreman assigned her to machine a chrome diameter and she was enormously discouraged when, after several hours, she still couldn't do it. It was a male friend who told her how he had caught the foreman laughing the next morning, telling his buddies how he had the girl apprentice trying to machine a chrome diameter when everyone (every journeyed machinist, that is) knows it can't be done. You have to grind a chrome diameter. He kept up this kind of harassment, aimed specifically at her because of her gender, until evenutally she quit. He never mentioned sexual availability once. He didn't have to.

It is not hard to understand why it is so difficult for most women to handle sexual and gender harassment. Too many of us have internalized the message that if you are nice to everyone, they will be nice to you. So when we wander into territory that has been male-dominated for a thousand years, where we don't know the language, the mechanical skills or the style of working, where we're negotiating a minefield of potential disasters, both large and small, mechanical and personal, it seems even more important to be nice - just to survive on a daily basis. It is also harder to summon up the confidence to be assertive, speak up and demand that the harasser stop.

Traditions

There are two issues here. One is that it takes some of us a long time to speak up. This is something women are working at and teaching each other with assertiveness training and life skills classes to build our confidence.

The other involves looking at the male side, where the harassment is coming from. In other words, look at the traditionally male, blue collar workplace from a male, blue collar perspective. In a workplace traditionally dominated by men, it is vital to remember that *harassment in the trades did not start when women came on the job*. Men in the blue collar workplace have always harassed each other, and continue to do so, for two reasons. (I am not, for a minute, excusing harassing behaviour, but it can be useful to understand where it comes from.)

In the first place, there is a strong tradition of harassing the apprentice or rookie on the job. If you ask a tradesman why he is harassing some apprentice (it's always a weaker, smaller target), the journeyman will reply, "Because someone did it to me."

Secondly, for many men harassment is a means of testing the mettle or the temper of their workmates. I have seen men harass a male or female co-worker mercilessly until the object of harassment finally got up the nerve (or the fury) to tell him to "f--- off!" And then, to their amazement, he turned into a charming, likeable workmate. He just wanted to know where they drew their own personal line, and he pushed until he found it. It's always been that way.

The Pack Mentality

Perhaps the tradition of harassment will diminish or end when there are enough women and gentle men and gay and lesbian people in the trades to break it. But the tradition and habits of harassment are complicated by what I consider to be a much more frightening situation: the unwillingness of men, and not just women, to speak out against harassment.

I have found that almost any man will treat me fairly in a one-on-one situation, but if you put several men together in a construction shack a strange thing can happen. They will not criticize the most outrageous behaviour of their colleagues. In fact, they will often egg each other on. If you separate them, most of them will again become reasonably considerate individuals. Women call it the "pack" mentality.

I have no idea why this happens. Perhaps it is an upbringing that stresses status and competitiveness for men. Perhaps it is all those years of team sports which bonds them in some way.

I think it will not be a woman who explains this behaviour. All I know is that it damages both women and men. Harassment on the job will not end until individual men start speaking up.

It came as a revelation when I finally figured this out. I had been on a crew for a month, building one of the stations on the Vancouver Skytrain system. We got along well and I loved the work and working with my partner. As a crew, at lunch-times and breaks, we had broken out of the sports/drinking conversational ghetto and talked about food and family and news.

Then we got a new foreman who did everything he could to separate me and my partner. We ignored him. He gave us incorrect instructions and then blamed me when the work had to be redone. My partner spoke to the general superintendent. Finally, in the shack one day, the foreman started to tell a joke about rape. I found myself wilting in shame and humiliation and guilt. When he finished telling the joke, you could hear the flies buzzing at the windows. No one moved and no one laughed. He snorted, "None of you has any sense of humour!" and left. I could have kissed every one of the men in the shack that day.

What I had learned is that a harasser needs allies; that even if they only snicker or nod, they are accomplices. Every one of those men knew what the foreman wanted, but they chose to stand beside me and refused to go along with his "joke."

Breaking the Silence

Refusing to speak is one thing. Actually speaking up and countering another man is another. Only once in 15 years did a man actively speak up in my defence.

I was being ignored and undermined by the labourer assigned to me. This day, as we came out of the lunch shack, he made one more derogatory comment as he passed. By coincidence, the foreman was right behind me. "Lay off, Al!" he said. That was all, but it was as if trumpets had blared and God had descended to surround me with cherubim and seraphim waving protective swords. All of us knew exactly the impact of those few words. That labourer didn't say a word to me for weeks after, but I had everything I asked for, right away, like everyone else on the job.

Until the terrible "bonds" that men define as "loyalty" to one another, or as "team play," are put aside, women, visible minorities, aboriginal and gay and lesbian people will continue to be harassed and have to combat harassment on their own. This is what we mean when we tell men that it is time to end their silence. Isn't it ironic that the hard work of sticking our necks out, defying tradition and speaking out turn out to be the same for all of us, men and women!

Sexual Harassment in the Legal Profession

Paule Gauthier

Paule Gauthier served as President of the Canadian Bar Association for 1992-93. She is a partner in the Quebec law firm of Desjardins, Ducharme, Stein, Monast.

Sexual harassment exists in the legal profession. The legal community has generally assumed that sexual harassment was not a real problem in the profession and that, if it existed at all, it was an exceptional occurrence. But recent studies have shown that not only does sexual harassment occur in the legal profession, it is also a widespread and serious problem.

The experience of female law students, lawyers, law professors and judges should not be surprising; the legal profession reflects the same trends found in society as a whole. Yet it is profoundly disturbing that the perpetrators should be themselves guardians of the justice system. How can women believe that their complaints of sexual harassment will be heard, understood and dealt with in an appropriate manner when they know that their lawyers and judges may themselves be guilty of harassment?

This article examines the sexual harassment experienced by women within the legal profession and proposals for its eradication. While the focus is on the legal profession and the specific problems faced by women lawyers, the comments may be applicable to other sectors of the work force.

The Current Situation

Women face barriers to successful participation in the legal profession because of discrimination based on sex. The broad parameters of this gender bias within the profession are beginning to be understood. Studies have shown that barriers to equality include: salary differentials, difficulties obtaining articles, difficulties in securing good files and problems with work allocation, the lack of women in management and leadership positions, segregation into certain areas of practice, an unwillingness to accommodate female parents who have family responsibilities, and sexual harassment.[1]

Six provincial law societies, the regulatory bodies for the profession, have established inquiries into the status of women in the legal profession.[2] In addition, the national professional association, the Canadian Bar Association, established a Task Force on Gender Equality in August 1991 chaired by former Supreme Court of Canada Justice, the Honourable Bertha Wilson. The mandate of the Task Force was to inquire into and make recommendations on the improvement of the status of women within the legal profession. Its terms of reference were very broad, engaging women in all sectors of the practice, in large and small law firms, corporate counsel, government lawyers, professional organizations, in the law faculties, and in the judiciary. The Task Force reported in August 1993.

Five provincial law societies have surveyed their members on gender-related issues and reported on their findings. The results forcefully demonstrate the prevalence and seriousness of the problem of sexual harassment. Sexual harassment occurs in job interviews, in courtrooms and other professional settings. It is perpetrated by colleagues, clients and judges. The greatest problems occur where women are the most powerless and vulnerable. Many women face sexual harassment early in their careers as articled students and junior lawyers.

The overall results of the surveys are staggering.

For example, in Alberta, 31.5 percent of the women and 6 percent of the men responding to the survey reported having observed unwanted sexual advances being made against women lawyers by other lawyers in the last two years. Similar behaviour by clients against women lawyers was witnessed by 34.6 percent of the women and 8.2 percent of the men. In addition, almost two-thirds of the women (64.7 percent) and one-third of the men (32.1 percent) reported having observed women lawyers being the butt of unwanted teasing, jokes and comments of a sexual nature made by male lawyers. More than half of the women, but only 18.2 percent of the men, had observed such behaviour being directed at women lawyers by their clients. The survey also confirmed the existence of sexual harassment by judges. It ranged from unwanted sexual advances to unwanted teasing, jokes or comments of a sexual nature. Other respondents indicated that they had heard comments from judges which, while not overtly sexual, were nonetheless sexist and patronizing.

The results are depressingly similar in the British Columbia study. Of the women respondents, 33.7 percent reported observing or experiencing the most obvious forms of sexual harassment (unwanted sexual advances) against a woman lawyer by another lawyer at least once during the last two-year period, and 28.7 percent reported observing this form of sexual harassment directed at support staff. Of the male respondents, 10 percent reported observing unwanted sexual advances towards women lawyers by other lawyers, and 16.7 percent reported observing sexual harassment of support staff at least once during the same period. With respect to "unwanted teasing, jokes or comments of a sexual nature," 68.2 percent of women respondents reported observing this form of sexual harassment of women lawyers by other lawyers, and 48 percent of women respondents observed it with respect to support staff.

Male respondents also reported observing such behaviour directed at women lawyers (34.5 percent) and support staff (29.3 percent) at least once during the two years prior to the survey.[3]

The surveys also show that sexual harassment can have very serious consequences including acute emotional, physical and social stress for the employee and a substantial cost to the employer in terms of lost productivity, turnover, and reputation.

Women respondents to the surveys reported that sexual harassment has created a demeaning and humiliating work environment, affected their chances for promotion and, in some cases, has caused them to leave the firm or give up the practice of law altogether.

Even where personal comments were perceived by the female lawyer to be "innocent," they still had a negative impact. For example, comments about appearance were seen as trivializing the individual and as undermining her credibility and self-confidence. Some respondents went further and recounted how inappropriate gender-related comments could be used in professional settings as a tactic for exercising control over women.

One incident which has gained some prominence within the legal community illustrates this last point. It occurred when a female lawyer asked an opposing male counsel what his position would be with respect to the issue at hand. In the presence of the woman's client and other lawyers, the opposing counsel responded "I prefer the missionary position." The woman lawyer recounted the impact of this statement in the following words:

> I was in the courtroom. I am a solicitor. Mr. X is a solicitor. My client is sitting beside me. I was asking him a question that is probably asked every day in a courtroom

by almost every lawyer: "What is your position?" This is what I received. I was rattled. I was embarrassed. I was angry....

There was no question in my mind that this was sexual harassment. He looked blankly at me and he turned away. He did not say another thing to me....

He used these words as a weapon against me. That was the way he was defending his clients, by attacking me being a woman, and I am the counsel of record.[4]

The Structure of the Legal Profession

The structure of the legal profession poses a challenge to all those who would like to find solutions to the pervasive problem of sexual harassment. Lawyers are a self-regulating profession, and success within the profession is highly dependent upon professional relationships and solidarity with peers. These factors make it difficult for women even to report their experiences of sexual harassment and they limit the avenues for investigating and remedying complaints. As one woman was told, "If you make this issue public, you're stupid because you are jeopardizing your career."

Solutions

The profession is now struggling to find the means to eradicate the problem of sexual harassment.

The Law Society of British Columbia has concluded that the

following steps have to be taken in order to eradicate sexual harassment:

> the legal profession must recognize that sexual harassment is a serious impediment to a woman's ability to participate equally in the practice of law;

> sexual harassment must not be condoned by employers;

> there must be realistic means of redress.

The law societies of Ontario and British Columbia are taking the lead in getting the profession to deal with sexual harassment. The three main avenues for change are:

> the adoption of statements of principles on sexual harassment;

> the creation of appropriate procedures for the investigation and redress of complaints of sexual harassment; and

> the establishment of education programs on sexual harassment.

In addition to the recognition that sexual harassment is a serious and pervasive problem, changes must occur at a number of levels: behavioural, attitudinal and institutional.

To bring about such change, there must be an understanding of the kind of conduct that may constitute sexual harassment. This is important because women and men tend to perceive behaviour differently. Even well-intentioned compliments by co-workers or supervisors can form the basis of a cause of action if a "reasonable woman" would consider this conduct as amounting to sexual harassment. At its core, sexual harassment is based on the inability of some men to relate to women as individuals. As Bertha Wilson commented in a speech delivered at the 1992 Annual Meeting of the Canadian Bar Association, some men can only relate to women "socially and sexually" but not on a professional level.

The great divide between the perceptions of men and women is one of the greatest challenges, so emphasis must be placed on education and communication. Employers must recognize the seriousness of the situation and be prepared to act. Progress will be made when a firm is prepared to sanction or even dismiss a top-billing lawyer who sexually harasses a woman.

Human rights legislation and human rights commissions are seen as less effective in dealing with sexual harassment in the legal profession. As a self-regulating profession, the legal profession sees its priorities as developing internal policies and procedures which include:

- definitions of sexual harassment, including lists of examples of inappropriate behaviour;

- policies which are to be applied regardless of status or seniority;

- mechanisms for complaints, using an adviser either within or outside the firm;

- informal resolution mechanisms to make it easier to complain in cases of less serious forms of sexual harassment;

- investigation procedures that are confidential and fair;

- strict disciplinary measures;

- reports by colleagues who witness sexual harassment;

- ▸ communication of policies;

- ▸ checklists for ensuring compliance with the policy.

In addition, firms and other employers should provide training programs for their personnel. Such training should include: (1) special training for those who will be responsible for implementing the policy; (2) regular training for all administrative staff, associates and partners to explain and discuss the problem of workplace harassment and the firm's policy; and (3) training as part of orientation for new employees.

The eradication of sexual harassment requires action by law societies, bar associations, law firms and other employers and all members of the profession. Reform must occur within the context of the relationship between sexual harassment and other forms of discrimination against women in the workplace. The first steps have been taken towards recognizing the problem, but many challenges lie ahead as the legal profession faces these issues. Fundamental change is essential and will have beneficial outcomes both within the profession and on the justice system as a whole.

Notes

1. Sheila Martin, *The Dynamics of Exclusion: Women in the Legal Profession* (1992), a paper prepared for the CBA's Task Force on Gender Equality Conference.

2. Ontario, British Columbia, Alberta, Saskatchewan, Quebec and Nova Scotia.

3. Law Society of British Columbia, *Gender Bias in the Justice System* (1992).

4. Id. at page 3.

Sexual Harassment - A View from the Universities

Barbara Whittington

Barbara Whittington is an associate professor in the School of Social Work, University of Victoria. She has been the harassment adviser at the university since 1985 and President of the Canadian Association against Sexual Harassment in Higher Education since 1990.

Sexual harassment is front page news. From personal disclosures to court decisions we are all learning about the damage this kind of unfair treatment can cause and the costs associated with it. Employers, unions and institutions such as universities are struggling to respond.

This paper will address the dynamics of sexual harassment on Canadian campuses and the formal and informal responses of the college and university communities. The mistakes we have all made - euphemistically called learning experiences - are helpful to share. As the Harassment Policy Adviser in a mid-size university (16,000 students), and as the President of the Canadian Association against Sexual Harassment in Higher Education, I have had the opportunity to consult with many colleges and universities, as well as with unions, government ministries and large and small businesses. In the position of adviser, my frontline duties have ranged from being the first point of contact for victims of harassment to designing policies, procedures and innovative educational programs. On a bad day,

---

I have viewed the university as a patriarchal institution that pays only lip-service to the idea of combatting sexual harassment. On a good day, I have still viewed the university as a patriarchal institution, but one struggling in a number of ways to change. This paper will look at those struggles.

Campus communities are places of work and study. For some who live in residence they are also temporary homes. Part of the population, the staff and faculty, remains stable over time while the student population changes annually. This fact needs to be carefully considered when promoting change in behaviour and attitudes through education. For example, if you institute a comprehensive educational program you may need to repeat it frequently, or target others to pass on the knowledge about harassment. Unlike a business where one can predict a 5 percent turnover of employees, the university system has a 15 to 25 percent change in population every year.

Universities are often compared to small towns, but the comparison is only valid if you also add that it is a small town whose leaders can tell you whether or not you can stay. This type of power, which faculty have over students, cannot be ignored.

The Scope of the Problem

Victims of sexual harassment in academia handle their experiences in a variety of ways. In the last reporting year [all statistics are from the University of Victoria Annual Report on Harassment, September 1991 to September 1992], the majority of complaints came from the student population. Of 101 complaints, 60 percent were from students. From studies comparing the number of students who have experienced sexual harassment with the number who lodged complaints, it is clear that there is significant under-reporting of harassment.

The statistics at the University of Victoria are similar to those I have reviewed from other Canadian institutions. The majority of complaints of harassment are from women (87 percent at UVic), and the majority of respondents - people accused of harassment - are men (90.4 percent at UVic). Students complain about harassment more frequently than staff or faculty. Close to student/faculty harassment is student/student harassment. The most common allegations are of sexist treatment through conduct, jokes and remarks.

The victims of harassment experience the range of reactions cited in research on rape. While each story is different, I have heard complainants say over and over again, "It's not fair"; "I didn't know what to do"; "I *should* have known what to do"; "I feel sick"; "I avoid going near that office"; "I thought he thought I was smart"; "I end up laughing so they'll treat me like one of the group." Frequently there are expressions of self-doubt, such as: "I should have seen it coming"; "I guess I didn't deserve that A"; "Maybe I should quit"; "Maybe I am too sensitive."

Issues for the Harassed: Accountability, Justice and Fear of Retribution

The relationship of professor to student can be seen as somewhat similar to that of employer to employee in terms of power. This power has obvious and subtle dimensions. A professor can not only pass or fail a student but can confer benefits or subtly penalize students as well. Students often need references or recommendations for future study; research opportunities, informal contacts, mentorships and teaching assistantships are some of the 'perks' that the student/professor relationship can bring or not. While people from outside the campus system may see a student as someone with many choices, in my experience students are extremely vulnerable, psychologically, professionally and economically.

Many students have returned to school and carry family or job responsibilities. Many are enrolled in programs or schools where competition for places is keen. The job market following graduation is extremely difficult. Students are dependent on faculty both for present assistance and for general future help. Often the areas of concentration are so narrow that there may be only one professor specializing in the student's chosen area of study. This creates the same dynamic as there is in the workplace during times of high unemployment. Students are in the position of having little choice if they are being harassed.

The two primary elements that form the core of the issue of harassment and appear to motivate victims of harassment to complain can be termed accountability and justice. In our current legal system discrimination has a very subjective component. Unlike theft or assault where the society clearly states its abhorrence of the crime, with discrimination through sexual harassment, the victim must first realize that someone has done something unfair. Since, as stated earlier, we know that very few victims of harassment ever report their story, I always ask: 1) What factors did you consider before you came and talked to me? 2) What do you think should happen?

The responses I receive to these two questions have implications for designing useful policy and procedures as well as implications for relevant educational programs. I will give just two examples. The most frequently cited responses to the questions "Why report now?" and "Why report at all?" generally relate to future potential victims of harassment. Complainants often look at the common good and decide that the dangers of not reporting harassment outweigh the very real negative consequences of reporting. While many victims of harassment initially react to the harassment at a very private personal level, they often come to the conclusion after a number of weeks or months that unless they say something or do something, another woman (usually) may encounter the same problem with the same person. The assurances of confidentiality, the complainant-driven component in the policy, and generous time limits for reporting are all examples of elements in policy and procedure that encourage reporting.

The second question - "What should happen?" - leads to educational and procedural initiatives. In a recent case, the complainant decided that she would not complain formally if the respondent seemed to understand the impact of the harassment and demonstrate this by becoming involved in workshops and plays designed to explore discrimination. The need for flexible and creative responses and resolutions is crucial.

Mediation in a form that addresses the power imbalances has proved successful in a number of cases of sexual harassment. Mediation in this situation is more like victim/offender reconciliation and is possible only when there is no dispute about what took place. However, it has not proved crucial to label such conduct as harassment at the very outset. The mediations that have been viewed by the victims as successful are those that conclude with a common understanding that the conduct of the harasser created a hostile working or educational environment for the complainant. The mediations that have been less successful are those where there is no such acknowledgment of wrongdoing. However, the private nature of these mediations can be counter-productive to the education of the campus community. Furthermore, on most campuses, the mediation option does not allow for enforceable sanctions or consequences.

If mediation is to be part of an informal resolution option, the mediator must be well informed about the dynamics of harassment and well trained in mediation involving power and gender issues.

Four out of five professors are male, while over half the student population is female. Many female students go through their entire university career without any professional contact with a female professor. The importance of this for role modelling and mentoring is obvious. The stereotype of the lecherous professor is sometimes a reality. The boundaries between students and professors can become blurred. The rules about professional ethics are often more difficult to adhere to in an environment where sexual harassment is confused with freedom of expression and academic freedom.

Sexual harassment complaints have arisen from supposedly consensual affairs between professors and students. While many campuses have begun to develop conflict of interest policies or professional ethics guidelines to discourage personal relationships between professors and students, management and staff, many such relationships do exist. The argument is sometimes made that personal, consenting relationships are no one else's business. However, conflicts often arise because of the perception of bias. For example, the professor may favour one student in awarding grades or a teaching assistantship and others see that as conferring a benefit not available to them. I often see the individuals in the harassment policy office when such seemingly consensual affairs end. The person with the least power - usually a woman, whether a student or junior faculty member - is suddenly put in a very vulnerable position. The person with the power has the potential to create a poisonous environment for his or her ex-lover. In one case, the professor did not want the relationship to end and when it did the student suddenly found that all her previous work was being questioned and that the conduct of everyday business became intolerable.

Models, Procedures and Personnel

Most universities and colleges now have part-time or full-time advisers who operate as a first contact for complaints of harassment. From 1985 to 1990, many institutions tried a committee model to field complaints. The committee, usually staff, faculty and students, would serve as a group of advisers, and the complainant could speak to any one of these contact people. In the light of experience, it has become obvious that this model has certain limitations. Accessibility, expertise and continuity were all problems that led most campuses to adopt a model of a single adviser after struggling with the committee model. Complainants want to speak with someone who is an expert in this area and someone who has the power to intervene if necessary. Consultations with unions, businesses and government suggest that they have encountered similar problems. There is an underestimation of the broad and deep level of expertise needed in dealing with harassment matters in an organization.

Most organizations have learned by hard experience what can happen when the complexity of a harassment case is underestimated. In reviewing the disputes that have reached the Supreme Court of Canada or have become human rights cases, all appear to involve missed opportunities for a less painful resolution. A clear policy, common-sense procedures, and competent advisers trained in issues of discrimination, mediation and investigation can often produce an early resolution of painful harassment matters. Of the 218 cases of harassment (sexual and general) at the University of Victoria during the last reporting period, 98.6 percent were resolved informally.

Looking Backwards to See Forwards: Mistakes and New Ideas

With experience, campus harassment advisers have changed many aspects of their work. We now know how to develop or revise a policy that people will read and use. We know of the ongoing debates about public reporting, how to work with the media and how to manage a hearing process that is fair and humane. We know that, small interventions can have a tremendous ripple effect. We know that when an allegation of harassment has become public, we need to have a public response. Departments and groups involved in the midst or the edge of a complaint often need an opportunity to debrief. How these debriefings are handled is crucial to re-establishing working relationships.

As advisers, we need to link complainants with each other to further their healing. Respondents need to know what rights they have and be connected with their union or association, if they have one. Hearing panels must devise creative resolutions or sanctions. If an employee of the university is suspended without pay, why should that money go to the institution instead of the complainant? We know that, unless the senior administration actively supports the efforts of the policy, one might as well not have a policy.

The power differences inherent in the structure of the university create fertile ground for abuse such as discrimination through harassment. The time for being a "good sport" has passed.

Sexual Harassment -- Assisting the Victim

Yvonne Séguin

Yvonne Séguin is a co-founder of Le Groupe d'aide et d'information sur le harcèlement sexuel au travail de la province de Québec incorporée.

Introduction

The Groupe d'aide et d'information sur le harcèlement sexuel au travail de la province de Québec incorporée is the only organization in Quebec and, it seems, in Canada, that specializes in the problem of sexual harassment in the workplace.

Twelve years ago, when the Groupe was established, the issue of sexual harassment was shrouded by a veil of silence. A woman who was sexually harassed found herself with nowhere to go for information, help and support. The Quebec Commission on Human Rights provided a channel for legal action, but there was no one to help the victim through the process; no one who could validate her experience or understand her pain.

The Groupe was set up by volunteers to provide information and support to victims of sexual harassment. In a very short time it was obvious that the Groupe was filling a real need because the calls started coming in for advice and help. Before long, weekly evening meetings turned into a full-time job.

We have dealt with thousands of cases over the years and have expanded our role and mandate from simply providing information and support for the victims to adopting an active role in the resolution of cases and initiating education and training for employers and others.

We provide services in two main areas: complaints and information.

Complaints

This service is provided free of charge and consists of technical and moral support.

When a victim of sexual harassment contacts our office, we will call the employer to see whether the situation can be resolved informally. If the victim has already resigned, we ask that she be reinstated, that the harasser be transferred out of the unit and, most important, that there be an acknowledgement that sexual harassment has occurred. Sometimes we suggest a training session on the problem of sexual harassment for all employees in the firm.

If an informal resolution is not possible, we help the victim put together a file which she can use when confronting the harasser and/or the employer, when meeting with the union or the Quebec Commission on Human Rights, or in court.

Throughout the process, we provide moral support to the victim through informal meetings and group and individual therapy sessions.

All our activities are designed to help the victim regain control of the situation and of her life.

Information

We hold awareness sessions, which are open to anyone, to demystify the concept of sexual harassment in the workplace and inform people of how they can stop or prevent it without taking legal action.

We also offer training sessions ("How to handle sexual harassment cases"; "How to investigate sexual harassment complaints"), which are adapted to participants' individual needs.

Since 1990, we have provided our expertise as consultants to private, public and parapublic organizations, unions, educational institutions, and community centres that wish to develop a policy on sexual harassment in the workplace.

Myths about Sexual Harassment

After having spoken to and counselled thousands of victims of sexual harassment, we have come to the conclusion that there is still a great misunderstanding of what sexual harassment is and is not and of the devastating consequences it can have on the woman being victimized - and it almost always is a woman. Among all cases we have had, only six involved a male victim. Five of these men had been harassed by other men and only one by a woman.

Many myths about sexual harassment persist in the workplace. Among these myths are that

(i)   "flirtation" and "sexual harassment" are one and the same.

Anyone who has lived through the experience of sexual harassment knows she was not simply the subject of innocent flirtation. Flirting is a social activity practised between consenting partners. Sexual harassment implies absence of consent.

(ii)   sexual harassment is the result of provocation by the victim.

Numerous studies have demonstrated that, in a large proportion of cases of sexual harassment in the workplace, the harassment is not triggered by physical attraction. Rather, it seems that it is primarily a need by the harasser to abuse his power that triggers such incidents.

(iii) women frequently make false accusations of sexual harassment.

In our experience, very few false accusations are made in the workplace. Given the psychological, social and economic consequences for the victim of launching a complaint, no woman embarks on this route lightly.

(iv) sexual harassment cannot arise from a single act; it requires persistent and repeated conduct.

It is true that if the approach is subtle, it can often be difficult to identify sexual harassment as such unless the incident is repeated. Nevertheless, it must be specified that the more obvious or crude the approach, the less need there is for it to be repeated in order to identify it correctly as sexual harassment.

(v)   sexual harassment is not a serious matter; women should learn to just ignore men who behave in this manner in the workplace.

This, perhaps, is the most serious and damaging myth. The assumption that "boys will be boys" and one has to expect and accept this means that society does not see or understand what sexual harassment really is and the affect it has upon women.

We must learn, once and for all, to make the distinction between social conditioning and natural behaviour. A harasser's behaviour is not caused by his glands, but by a social upbringing in which women are not respected.

Until these and other myths are debunked, it will be hard to make real progress in eradicating sexual harassment from the workplace.

The Consequences of Sexual Harassment on the Victim

Over the years, we have seen the devastating effects that sexual harassment in the workplace can have on women's lives.

From the moment a woman objects to having to live with such a situation, she is confronted with a whole series of obstacles.

Most of the time, the victim finds that there is no one to take her side. Too often, her employer does not take her seriously, her union refuses to become involved if the complaint concerns two union members, and her colleagues ostracize her because she is seen as a troublemaker who can't take a joke. If she persists in trying to have her rights respected, she exposes herself to retaliation of all kinds: threats, overwork, pressure to withdraw the complaint, a transfer or demotion with a loss in wages, creation of a disciplinary record, constant surveillance.

Gradually, she loses interest in her work, her performance suffers as a result, and she is away from work more and more frequently. She starts to think about abandoning her career or job, which she used to enjoy. On some occasions, the victim decides to pursue a different career altogether and may even refuse to re-enter the labour market for a certain period of time, perhaps for quite a while. Too often, she is fired or forced to resign.

The accumulated stress can lead to serious physical problems, such as extreme nervousness, insomnia, heartburn, ulcers, digestive problems, persistent headaches, allergies, high or low blood pressure, dehydration caused by very serious diarrhoea, and weight loss. In rare cases, the tension is so extreme that it causes incontinence and, in very exceptional cases, suicide attempts. The longer the sexual harassment persists, the more physical effects are felt.

There are also serious financial consequences. Absences from work become more frequent, resulting in lost wages. If the victim takes sick leave, the required processing time causes delays, and bills start to pile up.

Action requiring legal advice or the services of a lawyer causes further debts, and the tensions between the victim and her partner become even more difficult to bear.

The victim's morale is at its lowest, and she gradually sinks into depression. She feels humiliated, powerless and frustrated. She starts feeling guilty, and begins to question her own actions. Did I provoke the harasser? Was I right to complain? Did I say something? Did I do something? I'm sure that I'm not in the wrong, but what is happening? Why me?

The victim asks herself all these questions hundreds of times. She questions her own actions, but can find no answer. Sometimes, she even begins to doubt her own sanity. The situation becomes unbearable. She finds herself at a dead end, without any moral support, and depression takes hold.

As the stress increases, the victim's home life starts to deteriorate as well. It is more difficult to deal with the children, and almost impossible not to lose patience with them. The victim's partner no longer recognizes the person who is sharing his life; she is always in a bad mood and no longer wants to do anything.

Sexual relations become more and more infrequent or cease altogether. The stress in the workplace, the off-colour jokes and innuendoes, kill any desire for lovemaking. The partner, who is not responsible for what the victim is experiencing at work, is nevertheless the first one to suffer the consequences. The victim's lack of desire affects the partner as well, who no longer knows how to react.

The longer the sexual harassment persists, the more it affects the victim and the more the life of the couple deteriorates. In many cases, the relationship is shattered, and sometimes separation or divorce are the only possible solutions.

The victim is no longer the same person. She has lost her career, her safety, her family and her health, all because of sexual harassment.

Conclusion

In the first years of the Groupe d'aide's existence, few employers were interested in the problem of sexual harassment in the workplace. They preferred to refer to it as a personal problem, rather than a personnel problem.

There is evidence that employers are becoming increasingly aware that sexual harassment is both more prevalent and more serious than they had previously thought.

They are starting to understand that sexual harassment in the workplace literally poisons the work environment. It affects the victim physically, morally, psychologically and financially, and can have serious repercussions for the harasser as well. Everyone's work and performance are affected. Sexual harassment results in financial losses to employers and to society in general.

Society must accept that sexual harassment is a serious social problem. It is a form of social and sexual control which breeds fear and insecurity in the face of potential violence, and which tends to keep its victims in a state of submission. We must change people's behaviour, denounce intolerance and indifference, and foster respect for oneself and for the people around us.

Section III

Legal Rights and Obligations

When "No" Isn't Enough: Sexual Harassment and the Canadian Human Rights Act

Michelle Falardeau-Ramsay

Michelle Falardeau-Ramsay is Deputy Chief Commissioner of the Canadian Human Rights Commission, a position she has held since 1988. Her previous appointments include Chair of the Immigration Appeal Board and Deputy Chair of the Public Service Staff Relations Board.

A secretary complains that her manager runs his hands along her side when she stands at the filing cabinet. He refers to her as his "sexatary" and repeatedly asks her about her sex life.

A female staff member is subjected to negative comments about her appearance by her male co-workers, who call her "fat cow" and say "waddle, waddle" when she walks by and "swish, swish" to imitate the sounds of her nylons when she walks.

A woman who is employed as a mechanical engineer constantly faces sexist remarks, such as "this is a man's job" and "a woman's place is in the kitchen." She is also grilled about her bathroom habits. Posters of nude women are up on the walls.

For many of us, these are practically unimaginable situations. But according to an Angus Reid/Southam News survey

---

conducted in October 1991, 37 percent of women and
10 percent of men who work outside the home say sexual
harassment in the workplace is a reality they have encountered.

Harassment is illegal under section 14 of the *Canadian Human
Rights Act*. The Act prohibits discriminatory practices -
including harassment - in employment and the provision of
services on such grounds as race, sex, marital and family status.
In 1992, the Commission received 208 harassment complaints;
approximately 63 percent or 128 actual cases were for sexual
harassment.

The Act covers employees of all federal departments, agencies,
Crown corporations and industries under federal jurisdiction,
such as banks, interprovincial transportation companies, telecommunications firms, and certain mining operations. It also
protects anyone who obtains a service from any of these bodies.

The Commission has developed a policy statement providing
examples of the types of behaviour that could constitute
harassment, such as:

- verbal abuse or threats;
- unwelcome remarks, jokes, innuendoes, or taunting
  about a person's body, attire, sex, age, marital status,
  ethnic or national origin, religion, etc.;
- displaying pornographic, racist, or other offensive
  or derogatory pictures;
- practical jokes which cause awkwardness or
  embarrassment;
- unwelcome invitations or requests, whether indirect
  or explicit, or intimidation;
- leering or other gestures;
- condescension or paternalism which undermines
  self-respect;

- ▶ unnecessary physical contact, such as touching, patting, pinching, or punching; and
- ▶ physical assault.

In its 1989 decision in *Janzen and Govereau v. Platy Enterprises*, the Supreme Court of Canada broadly defined sexual harassment as "unwelcome conduct of a sexual nature, which detrimentally affects the work environment, or leads to adverse job-related consequences for victims of harassment." In addition, Chief Justice Dickson made it clear that sexual harassment also encompasses situations in which "no tangible economic rewards are attached to involvement in the behaviour." In other words, harassment can occur even if the victim's job or salary is not at stake.

Although most sexual harassment cases involve a male harassing a female, they can include a female harassing a male, as well as harassment by a member of the same sex. Nor is harassment limited to the actual workplace: it can occur on business trips, on training courses, and at staff parties. The legislation provides protection for harassment committed in any work-related situation during or outside normal business hours. It also provides protection to any member of the public using a federally regulated service, such as a bank or airline ticket office.

Harassment often affects job performance. For instance, it could interfere directly with the accomplishment of a particular task, or it could cause undue stress or stress-related illness which might also affect performance. In addition, poor performance reviews might be the result of not submitting to a harasser's demands. In one case that came before the Commission, a female manager complained that she was harassed by her immediate supervisor. She alleged he kept her late at work for discussions about his personal life, pressed his pelvic area up against her chair, and touched her breasts.

Shortly after she complained in writing, her supervisor started excluding her from meetings. He gave her a poor performance evaluation. She then became ill because of the stress, her work suffered and her employment was terminated.

For victims, the cost of harassment is usually high, both financially and in terms of their mental and physical well-being. Many sexual harassment cases follow the same pattern. A woman, who is acknowledged to be a good worker, is harassed. The resulting stress causes health problems and health-related absences. She finally resigns on her doctor's orders or is let go because of her frequent absences or because her work has deteriorated due to the stress. By this time, the woman can have a significant stress-induced illness, a lack of self-esteem, and no job. Many harassment victims require professional assistance in order to be able to lead normal lives again.

Organizations, too, can suffer the effects of an environment that allows harassment. In a speech in January 1992, Douglas Baldwin, Senior Vice-President of Imperial Oil, estimated that sexual harassment costs the company almost $8 million per year in absenteeism, employee turnover, and lost productivity.

But even more important, sexual harassment is against the law, and organizations have a legal obligation to address harassment in the workplace. In the landmark case of *Robichaud v. Canada (Treasury Board)*, which was the first harassment case to go before the Supreme Court of Canada, a female supervisor of a team of cleaners with the Department of National Defence was sexually harassed by her foreman. The Department failed to remedy the situation, leading the Supreme Court of Canada to state that an employer has a positive responsibility to provide a work environment that is free of harassment.

In spite of this 1987 ruling, not all employers are taking the issue seriously. A 1991 survey by the Hudson Institute found that only 55 percent of organizations surveyed had a sexual harassment policy, and only one in five provided any supervisory training on harassment issues.

An employer who is concerned about providing a harassment-free workplace will take action both to prevent harassment and to deal with it when it occurs. This means developing a written policy on harassment and circulating it to all employees. The policy should make it clear that harassment will not be tolerated, and that disciplinary action will be taken against anyone who harasses another employee. Equally important, the policy should provide a clear and simple procedure for reporting and investigating incidents of harassment, and it should name the person or persons who should be contacted.

It is usually when an internal policy is lacking, or has not been properly implemented, that complaints are brought to the Canadian Human Rights Commission.

Complaints are filed with one of the Commission's seven regional offices. Sometimes the Commission can help the complainant and the respondent agree upon an early resolution of the complaint. If not, a full investigation is launched and a report is prepared for review by the Commission. In making these decisions, Commissioners have five courses of action. They can:

- accept a settlement reached during the investigation;
- dismiss the case if the evidence does not support the allegation;
- send the case back for further investigation;
- designate a conciliator; or
- request that a tribunal be appointed.

A conciliator works closely with the complainant and the respondent to settle the complaint. When a settlement has been reached, it comes to the Commission for approval. If conciliation fails, a Human Rights Tribunal may be appointed. The tribunal functions in a manner similar to a court of law -- witnesses are heard and evidence is presented. The Commission usually represents the complainant at the tribunal, while the respondent may be represented by independent legal counsel.

Tribunals can order the harassment to stop and the victim to be reinstated. They can also award compensation for lost wages and damages for hurt feelings, as well as demand an oral and/or written apology to the victim. In many cases, the tribunal will order that a harassment education program be developed and implemented as part of the redress. Tribunal decisions can be appealed to a review tribunal or to a federal court, and ultimately to the Supreme Court of Canada.

Interestingly, since the *Robichaud* decision, sexual harassment cases are rarely referred to tribunals. Most are resolved at the conciliation stage or earlier and can involve financial compensation for the victim, the development of a corporate harassment policy, and disciplinary action against the harasser.

Certainly the key to eliminating sexual harassment is education. Educating people on what behaviour is inappropriate and why, and educating employers on how to deal quickly and appro- priately with harassment when it occurs. Staff from the Commission's regional offices give seminars and workshops on harassment, while headquarters staff provides guidance to employers concerned about putting in place effective harassment policies and procedures. Only by increasing awareness of harassment and its ramifications can we ultimately achieve its elimination.

Legal Remedies for Workplace Gender Harassment

Cornish Advocates

*The authors of this paper are Mary Cornish,
Laura Trachuk, Cindy Wilkey and Susan Ursel.
Cornish Advocates is a Toronto law firm specializing
in employment, human rights and women's issues.*

Women have probably always been sexually harassed whenever
they have had to come into contact with men to do their work.
However, the concept of "sexual harassment" is a legal one
dating from the twentieth century. In the 1970s, feminists
started to frequently name sexual harassment, particularly
in workplaces and educational settings, as something which
is or should be unlawful.[1]   We will use the term "gender
harassment" in this paper, as it better captures some of the kinds
of harassment experienced by women which are related to their
gender, but is not necessarily understood as "sexual."

Unlike other issues upon which the feminist movement has
focused, such as wife assault, or sex discrimination generally,
gender harassment has historically been discussed and understood (by those outside the movement) in terms of what is or is
not illegal. This is striking because gender harassment is really

*Women's Bureau,
Human Resources Development Canada*   *51*

a specific manifestation of sex discrimination. This has been problematic because one of the consequences of understanding gender harassment only in a legal context is that it is perceived that if actions are not "illegal" they are not harassment.

Furthermore, as a result of this focus on the legal issues related to gender harassment, there has not been significant public attention to it as a social problem. Instead, attention has come to the issue through the publicity of lawsuits, and employers have begun educational initiatives out of the fear of being "sued." One rarely, for example, hears any discussion or public condemnation of the gender harassment that women face every day on the street, on the transit system, etc.

As a result of this history, we usually discuss gender harassment in terms of concepts which have been adopted by courts and tribunals that have been mandated to interpret anti-discrimination legislation.

At first, the recognition of gender/sexual harassment focused on what is often referred to as "quid pro quo" harassment. This is the situation in which a person in a workplace who is in a position to confer or deny a benefit indicates that benefit will not be received or some negative consequence will ensue if a sexual advance is rejected. Subsequently, the recognition of gender/sexual harassment was expanded to include the concept of a poisoned work environment. "Poisoned work environment" included the idea that a person's work environment was detrimentally affected by the actions and attitudes of co-workers such as name calling, groping, pornographic pictures in the workplace, etc.

Sexual harassment was first recognized as being unlawful (and therefore was first recognized at all by many people) in Canada under some of the federal and provincial human rights codes.

Sexual harassment is included in the Ontario Code which states:

> 6(2) Every person who is an employee has a right to freedom from harassment in the workplace because of sex by his or her employer or agent of the employer or by another employee.
>
> (3) Every person has a right to be free from,
>
> (a) a sexual solicitation or advance made by a person in a position to confer, grant or deny a benefit or advancement to the person where the person making the solicitation or advance knows or ought reasonably to know that it is unwelcome; or
>
> (b) a reprisal or a threat of reprisal for the rejection of a sexual solicitation or advance where the reprisal is made or threatened by a person in a position to confer, grant or deny a benefit or advancement to the person.

Most of the codes which include sexual/gender harassment use very similar language. However, not all provincial human rights codes do specifically refer to gender or sexual harassment. For example, the Manitoba Code does not include it and as a result, in *Janzen and Platy Enterprises*[2], the employer, Platy Enterprises, argued that gender/sexual harassment was not illegal in Manitoba. A tribunal under the Manitoba legislation found that although the legislation did not specifically refer to sexual harassment it was a species of sex discrimination and therefore prohibited in the province. However, the Manitoba Court of Appeal agreed with the employer and rejected the Tribunal's decision. The decision was appealed to the Supreme Court of Canada. The Women's Legal Education and Action Fund (LEAF) intervened in the case to argue that the Manitoba law must be interpreted as including a prohibition against gender harassment under s.15 of the *Canadian Charter of Rights and Freedoms*. The Supreme Court agreed and provided a non-exhaustive definition of sexual harassment as follows:

> ...unwelcome conduct of a sexual nature that detrimentally affects the work environment or leads to adverse job related consequences for the victims of the harassment.

The deficiency in this definition is that it may not be interpreted as being wide enough to include the concept of "gender" harassment. This is unfortunate because, as noted above, sexual harassment is generally understood to include only actions which are illegal, and any behaviour which does not fall into this category is often not considered to be sexual harassment. However, the effect of the Supreme Court's decision is that "sexual" harassment at least is prohibited in all jurisdictions in Canada.

Most women who wish to take legal action against gender harassment in their workplace resort to the human rights commission in their jurisdiction. However, this has frequently proved to be an inadequate solution for many women. Problems stem from the under-resourcing of human rights commissions which have waiting lists of many years; from the commissions' strong emphasis on settlements which in the past have been protected from publication; and from human rights tribunals' conservatism with respect to remedies. Tribunals rarely order the reinstatement of women to positions they have left, been fired from or never received because of harassment, and financial remedies are most often in the range of $1,500 to $3,000. These amounts do not even come close to compensating women for the trauma of being harassed, not being believed and having to go through the entire human rights commission process to have their complaints recognized.

Tribunals seem to believe that ruling that harassment has occurred is their main purpose and compensating the women who have suffered it is secondary. As a result, compensation is often of a "symbolic" nature.[3] This is a misconception in our view: compensating the women who have suffered harassment is as important as finding that harassment occurred. Although women initially may make comments like "I do not care about the money I just want justice," they find that the small amounts that they are awarded undermine their victory in having their complaint upheld. Women perceive that the small awards they receive suggest that their injuries were minor and therefore that there was only a "little bit" of harassment. In fact, women who have been subjected to gender harassment often suffer "post-traumatic stress syndrome" an illness which manifests itself in many different ways: loss of appetite; inability to sleep; stomach cramps; diarrhoea; headaches; loss of self-esteem; inability to interact with others; suicidal thoughts.

This tendency to make "symbolic" compensation orders again reflects a limited recognition of sexual/gender harassment as only those acts which have been found to be illegal. It explains why boards and tribunals focus on the question of whether what has occurred is harassment and consider their role essentially complete once that determination is made.

In light of the inadequacy of the human rights process, women have recently sought to use other legal forums to address harassment situations. This is significant in terms of the historical understanding of harassment described above. If the community perceives that harassment has occurred only when a legal adjudicator has pronounced that a law has been breached, then more adjudicators pronouncing that more laws have been breached will expand the recognition of this fundamental problem of discrimination in our society.

In Ontario, a woman working for a large steel manufacturing plant was being subjected to ongoing and escalating gender harassment in her workplace. The harassment included actions such as name calling and exposing her to pornographic pictures as well as not having adequate washroom facilities and being required to clean the men's washroom. This worker was a member of a union and was elected to the workplace health and safety committee where she learned about her right to refuse unsafe work. She decided to exercise that right when she was forced to work with a co-worker who had been one of the sources of harassment. She argued that this was an unsafe work environment for two reasons: the stress caused by the harassment was making her ill; and the situation was so distracting that she had become concerned about her ability to work safely in such a hazardous environment. The employer took action against her and she filed a complaint with the Ontario Labour Relations Board.

This case was settled before the hearing was completed. Nevertheless, the ground has been laid for women who are being subjected to harassment which is causing or may cause them to become ill to complain to the occupational health and safety office in their jurisdiction or to exercise their right to refuse work. Furthermore, as the result of a subsequent complaint, the Occupational Health and Safety Branch in Ontario revised its policy with respect to the *Occupational Health and Safety Act* to recognize that it protects workers from dangerous "people" as well as dangerous "things."

Women are also seeking remedies under workers' compensation laws.

LEAF supported the fight of a 45-year-old black woman to establish entitlement to workers' compensation benefits for the psychological injury that she suffered as a result of years of sexual and racial harassment in the workplace. The woman worked in a predominantly white production facility and had advanced through several production lines to a "heavy packing" area that had historically been staffed only by men.

While on the line, she was subjected to overt sexualized racial harassment including the placing of images of black women performing sex acts for groups of white men at or near her work station. She was also subjected to less obvious harassment, in the form of active sabotage of her work by male co-workers and flagrant insubordination on the part of co-workers whose cooperation she required to ensure that production quotas were reached.

For several years the woman struggled to perform successfully in spite of the harassment, but the struggle took its toll. Finally, she suffered a severe psychological collapse when neither the company nor her union were prepared to support her complaint when a group of male co-workers placed a large carved soap penis on her packing line and stood around waiting for her to react.

When the woman applied for workers' compensation benefits she was turned down, first, because the Board did not believe her injury was caused by the workplace, and second, when medical evidence established the causal link beyond a doubt, because the Board would not recognize a purely psychological injury that did not have a physical injury at its root.

LEAF supported the woman's appeals through three levels within the Worker's Compensation Board. Concentrating first on the medical evidence, LEAF retained a clinical psychologist with expertise in sexual harassment to provide an assessment of the connection between the woman's injury and the workplace sexual harassment. This assessment provided powerful evidence of a direct causal link, but did not specifically deal with the racial elements of the harassment. To complete that part of the assessment, LEAF retained a second and equally powerful assessment from a psychiatrist who had expertise in the area of workplace injury and racism.

Once the medical evidence had been obtained, LEAF also retained a sociologist who is an expert in the study of racism and harassment. She prepared a report which combined a review of writing on the practice of systemic racism and harassment and an analysis of how those practices were at work in the woman's workplace.

An important part of the development of the case involved the use of a multidisciplinary committee to work with legal counsel to develop the way in which arguments dealing with the racial aspect of the harassment would be presented. The committee was almost exclusively composed of women of colour who, through training and experience, added an essential perspective to the analysis of the evidence and to the task of combining legal and sociological concepts of race and gender.

The appeals were successful and the woman became the first in Ontario to be awarded workers' compensation benefits for the effects of racial and gender harassment.[4] Recently the Workers' Compensation Appeals Tribunal held that a worker who was subjected at work to harassment based on gender and race was entitled to benefits.[5]

There has been considerable interest recently in the possibility of a civil action for gender harassment. It is not possible in Canada for a victim of harassment to "sue" the harasser and recover damages for a breach of a human rights code.[6] However, if gender harassing behaviour were to be included under an existing "tort," it might be possible to seek a remedy through the civil court process. One possibility would be to argue that gender harassment is "the intentional infliction of mental suffering" and can therefore give rise to a cause of action under that tort as it has in the U.S.[7] Another possibility which has been suggested is to sue for "breach of fiduciary duty," which has traditionally been used by employers against employees who they believe have breached their relationship of trust.

One other legal forum that women have been using for harassment situations is the criminal courts. If the harassment includes actual touching, one can ask the police to lay a charge of assault or, if that fails, one can attempt to prosecute the matter by appearing before a justice of the peace. Two other useful sections of the Criminal Code are 372(3), which prohibits harassing telephone calls, and 423(1)(f), which prohibits watching and besetting.

S.372(1) states:

> (3) Every one who, without lawful excuse and with intent to harass any person, makes or causes to be made repeated telephone calls to that person is guilty of an offence punishable on summary conviction.

S.423(1)(f) states:

> (1) Every one who wrongfully and without lawful authority, for the purpose of compelling another person to abstain from doing anything that he has a lawful right to do, or to do anything that he has a lawful right to abstain from doing,
>
> > (f) besets or watches the dwelling-house or place where that person resides, works, carries on business or happens to be,
>
> is guilty of an offence punishable by summary conviction.

S.372(1) therefore can be used in those not uncommon situations in which a woman is harassed by persistent telephone calls, and s.423(1)(f) can be used if harassment is taking the form of coming to one's home or work. It should be noted that the harassment need not take place in a work environment for these sections to be used.

Women's Bureau,
Human Resources Development Canada

Women are increasingly determined to have the harassment they experience recognized and eliminated. They are seeking legal avenues to assist them achieve these goals. Unfortunately, most legal remedies are limited to gender harassment in a work setting and cannot be used in other contexts. We need more discussion of gender harassment as an equality issue in society. Women are entitled to work and conduct their lives free of harassment. In the meantime, men who participate in these activities and employers who do not eradicate them from their workplaces will be facing increasingly frequent legal challenges.

Notes

1. See, for example, Backhouse, Constance, and Cohen, Leah, *The Secret Oppression: The Sexual Harassment of Working Women,* Toronto: McMillan, 1978, and MacKinnon, Catherine, *Sexual Harassment of Working Women: A Case of Sex Discrimination*, New Haven: Yale University Press,1979.

2. *Janzen v. Platy Enterprises Ltd.* [1989] 1 S.C.R. 1252 at 1284; (1989), 10 C.H.R.R. D/6205 at D/6227, para. 44451.

3. See for example the decisions published in the 1990 volumes of the Canadian Human Rights Reporter: *Wilgan and Davis v. Wendy's Restaurants of Canada Inc.* 11 C.H.R.R. D/119. Board found that the Complainants resigned at least in part because of the harassment they were subjected to. However they received only $750 and $1,125 respectively.

    Haight v. W.W.G. Management Inc. 11 C.H.R.R. D/124. Complainant received $8,720.

Blair v. Progressive Products Limited 11 C.H.R.R.
D/130. Complainant received $2,250.

Burridge v. Katsiris and Beef-Eaters Restaurant Ltd.
11 C.H.R.R. D/427. Complainant received $5,227.

Voeller v. Kingfisher Sales Inc. 11 C.H.R.R. D/433.
Board found that the Complainant had quit her job
because of the harassment. Complainant received
$3,800.

Dyson v. Pasin Plaster & Stucco Ltd. 11 C.H.R.R.
D/495. Board found that Complainant had been sexually
assaulted by her employer and quit as a result.
Complainant received $3,000.

McGregor v. McGavin Foods Limited 11 C.H.R.R.
D/15. Board found that Complainant had quit her job at
least partially because of the harassment. Complainant
received $3,116.

Korda v. PK and JP Enterprises Ltd. 11 C.H.R.R.
D/201. Board found that Complainant had quit her job
at least partially because of the harassment. Complainant
received $1,200.

*Ives v. Palfy (doing business as "The Public Market
Bakery"*) 11 C.H.R.R. D/483. Complainant received
$2,000.

4.   (Dec. 90/HO/636)

5.   Decision No. 636/91 21 W.C.A.T.R. 277

6. *Seneca College of Applied Arts and Technology and Bhadauria*, [1981] 2 S.C.R. 181.

7. See *Rogers v. Loews L'Enfant Plaza*, 526 F. Supp. 523 (D.D.C. 1981), *Shaffer v. National Can Corp.* 565 F. Supp. 909 (1983), *Howard University v. Best* 484 A. 2d 958 (D.C.App. 1984), and *Rice v. United Insurance Company of America* 465 So.1100 (Ala. 1984).

Legal Obligations of Employers and Unions to Protect Employees from Sexual Harassment

Arjun P. Aggarwal

Arjun P. Aggarwal, *former professor of human rights and industrial relations at Confederation College in Thunder Bay, Ontario, is the author of several books including* Sexual Harassment in the Workplace *(2nd edition 1992) and* Sexual Harassment: A Guide for Understanding and Prevention *(1992).*

Sexual harassment in the workplace has been ignored far too long. It is pervasive and is not an insignificant personnel issue as some people may believe. Sexual harassment will clearly be a major workplace issue for years to come and must be squarely faced by both public and private sector employers.

It is already evident that sexual harassment affects the well-being and economic livelihood of women employees, while also affecting the morale, productivity and integrity of the workplace. There are additional reasons it is essential that all employers should address the problem promptly. The majority of working age women are now in the labour force and their numbers are steadily growing.

Employers' Liability

Employers are responsible for objectionable sexual behaviour of their supervisors and managers. It is illegal for an employee's job, pay, promotion, demotion, layoff, discharge, or any other condition of employment to depend on a positive response to a supervisor's sexual advances or requests. It is forbidden by human rights law as unlawful sex discrimination.

It should be pointed out that employers may be held liable for their supervisors' behaviour even when they have forbidden such behaviour, and even when they do not know that such behaviour is taking place. In other words, under the rule of "strict liability" and "statutory liability," when supervisors (even co-workers) sexually harass employees the employer may be held liable, even if the employer had told the supervisor beforehand not to harass and even when the employer was unaware it was happening. The mere presence of policies prohibiting the misconduct and absence of knowledge of the misconduct are not sufficient to insulate the employer from liability. The employer's liability for sexual harassment committed by their supervisors is extensive.

The employer's liability for sexual harassment of its employees was clearly established by the Supreme Court of Canada in *Robichaud v. Canada (Treasury Board)*.[1] The Supreme Court determined that the *Canadian Human Rights Act* (and, for that matter, all human rights statutes) imposes a statutory duty on employers to provide a safe and healthy working environment, free of sexual harassment. The court stated that an employer could indeed be held liable under the Act for the actions of its employees.

It should be noted that the impact of the Supreme Court decision is not confined to employers under federal jurisdiction; employers in all jurisdictions are affected. The impact of the *Robichaud* decision may be briefly stated as follows:

i)   employers are responsible for the due care and protection of their employees' human rights in the workplace;

ii) employers are liable for the discriminatory conduct of, and the sexual harassment by, their agent and supervisory personnel;

iii) sexual harassment by a supervisor is automatically imputed to the employer when such harassment results in a tangible job-related disadvantage to the employee;

iv) explicit company policy forbidding sexual harassment and the presence of procedures for reporting misconduct may or may not be sufficient to offset liability.

Thus, an employer assumes absolute liability for acts of sexual harassment committed by its supervisory employees, regardless of whether the employer was aware, or should have been aware, of the discriminatory conduct.

An employer is also liable for sexual harassment by co-workers, but not to the same extent as for sexual harassment by supervisory personnel. An employer may also be held responsible for the acts of non-employees with respect to sexual harassment of employees in the workplace, where the employer or its agents or its supervisory employees knew or should have known of the unlawful conduct and the employer failed to take immediate and appropriate corrective action.

Employers have been found liable where the employer could be deemed responsible for creating the situation which caused or set in motion the sexual harassment; for example, where the employer forced the employees to wear sexy and revealing uniforms which made the employees subject to lewd comments, gestures, verbal and physical sexual harassment by customers and those passing through the lobby.

Liability for Hostile Work Environment

A hostile or poisonous work environment claim is a ground for action under human rights law. The employer would be liable if he or she knew, or should have known, of the alleged sexual harassment. If actual or constructive knowledge existed, and if the employer failed to take immediate and appropriate corrective action, the employer would be directly liable. Most commonly, an employer acquires actual knowledge by first-hand observation, or by the victim's internal complaint to supervisors or managers, or by a formal complaint of discrimination. Thus an employer is liable when it "knew or upon reasonably diligent inquiry should have known" of the harassment. Evidence of the pervasiveness of the harassment may give rise to an inference of knowledge or establish constructive knowledge.

Liability for "Off Hours" and "Off Premises" Harassment

Sexual harassment does not occur only in the course of employment, as would normally be expected. For example, it may take place when employees are out of the office, on a business trip, at an out-of-town conference, or at a company party or other function.

The Supreme Court of Canada in the *Robichaud* case has suggested that the phrase "in the course of employment" should be understood as meaning "work-related." Accordingly, the employer would be liable for sexual harassment of its employees, whether or not it takes place within office hours and whether or not it takes place on the employer's premises.

Protection of Female Employees in Non-Traditional Jobs

Women entering non-traditional jobs face unique problems. First, they face hostility from male employees. Women entering non-traditional jobs are expected to adjust and to tolerate a male-dominated work environment of sexual jokes, comments, teasing and more.

The evidence clearly indicates that in non-traditional jobs male employees often make it difficult for female employees to adjust to and feel comfortable in their jobs.

Sexual harassment in this context is employment discrimination by means of blackmail and/or a comprehensive pattern of hostile behaviour meant to underscore women's differences from and, by implication, inferiority to the dominant male group. It is the systemic, arbitrary abuse of male power and authority to extract sexual favours, to remind women of their ascribed inferior status, and to deprive them of employment opportunities and equality.

Employers thus have a special responsibility to oversee the fair and equitable adjustment of women entering non-traditional jobs. It is suggested that employers in such circumstances should anticipate such hostility, and should be aware of and sensitive to the concerns and difficulties female employees may face in non-traditional jobs. These employers should have a specifically designed plan of action to protect female employees from hostility and sexual harassment in the workplace.

Sexual Harassment Policy

Effective sexual harassment policies indeed decrease employers' vulnerability to litigation and its costs. Generally, good policies encourage the harassed employees to come forward and take action against the alleged harasser, giving management an opportunity to take prompt and effective action. Careful attention should be given to drafting and carrying out a policy that victims believe will provide effective redress, protect them from retaliation and educate all employees about the importance of this issue.

Unions' Obligations

Unions have not only a social and moral obligation, but also a legal duty to negotiate for a healthy and safe work environment for all their members. They also have an implied obligation to protect these rights that are guaranteed by the law of the land. Thus, the fight against discrimination in employment, including sexual harassment, cannot be contracted out by the unions, even if they so desire. In 1985, the Quebec Superior Court in *Foisy v. Bell Canada*[2] held that a union can agree to a settlement of wrongful dismissal of an employee, but it could not agree to settle an employee's claim for personal injury. In that case, the employer's failure to recognize and accept the behaviour as sexual harassment led to the employee's dismissal. Although the employee was subsequently reinstated with full back wages, through the grievance procedure, the court awarded her damages for personal injuries, such as humiliation and loss of self-respect, caused by the sexual harassment and wrongful dismissal.

Sexual harassment of union members by co-workers poses a serious dilemma for the unions. When members grieve each other's action, both parties, the victim and the harasser, are entitled to representation by the union.

If there is a sexual harassment clause in the collective agreement and the victim's claim against the co-worker is grievable, then the union is duty-bound to file a grievance on behalf of the victim. But at the same time, the union would find itself providing representation for and defending the harasser who is also a griever. It is not a very happy situation for the union.

However, unions do have a responsibility to prevent sexual harassment both in the workplace and in their organizations.

It is suggested that to protect their members from sexual harassment, the unions should develop a comprehensive strategy and plan, which may include the following:

1. Negotiating a sexual harassment clause in the collective agreement including grievance procedures and arbitration.

2. Providing support to the victim.

3. Educating members and shop stewards on sexual harassment through seminars and conferences.

4. Encouraging women to participate in union activities.

5. Conducting research and surveys on sexual harassment.

6. Political action lobbying against sexual harassment alone or with other unions or women's organizations.

7. Cooperating with employers in developing and implementing sexual harassment policy and procedures.

8. Developing their own sexual harassment policy and code of conduct for their own members and officers.

Moreover, it should be made clear that unions will not support members sexually harassing other workers.

Conclusion

If the participation of women in the work force is to be encouraged, gender insults, horseplay and sexual harassment must be eradicated from the workplace. That responsibility rests equally with employers and unions. If they are truly committed to this objective, employers and unions must cooperate to develop stringent rules which will deter the perpetration of sexual harassment. They cannot shirk their responsibility, nor can they expect a miraculous solution from the arbitrators - unless they give them a strong mandate to deal with the problem. The following four suggestions may be of use in such cases.

The parties (employer and union) need to make a special provision in the collective agreement specifically for the handling of discipline in sexual harassment cases. Some parties do this, especially in Western Canada.

Arguably, the parties could provide in the collective bargaining agreement that if sexual harassment by the griever is established, the arbitrator shall not interfere with the penalty imposed by the employer. This, however, would appear to be a very restrictive clause which would deny the griever the benefit of procedural due process, any mitigating circumstances and the concept of progressive discipline.

In addition, the parties may authorize an arbitrator, in the case of a victim's grievance, to order the transfer or removal of a supervisor - a harasser.

The arbitrator may also be authorized to order an apology in appropriate cases. An apology itself is not compensation, but it has some therapeutic value in healing the victim.

Notes

1.   *Robichaud v. Canada (Treasury Board)* (1987), 8
     C.H.R.R. D/4326 (S.C.C.) See also *Janzen v. Platy
     Enterprises Ltd.* (1989), 10 C.H.R.R. D/6205 (S.C.C.)

2.   (1985), 6 C.H.R.R. D/2817 (Que. Sup. Ct)

Section IV

**Employers' Perspectives
and Initiatives**

A Cooperative Approach to Combatting Sexual Harassment in the Workplace

Marlene Gallant

Marlene Gallant is Director of Human Rights, Employment Equity, Selection and Staffing at Bell Canada. She chairs Bell Canada's human rights complaint committee and co-chairs the company's joint union-management employment equity committees.

Sexual harassment in the workplace has existed as long as men and women have worked together because of the power and authority our society has traditionally awarded to men. Most experts agree that, while sexuality may be the focus, the real issue in harassment situations is power: who has it, how it is used, and against whom it is exercised. When men almost completely dominated the workplace (both in numbers and in power), sexual harassment might have occurred, but it was not much of an issue.

However, as women's participation in the labour force escalated during the 1960s and 1970s, society and the business community were forced to confront sexual harassment and acknowledge it as an important issue affecting a rapidly growing segment of the work force. A woman's right to a workplace free from harassment was acknowledged. Throughout the 1980s and early 1990s, the participation of women in the work force continued to increase, as did the numbers of women occupying positions of power and authority, as well as positions in traditionally male domains.

In the 1990s, since women are represented throughout the work force, they are more than ever prepared to identify and seek redress for instances of unacceptable behaviour, especially sexual harassment. Painful though the process may be to the individual, today's working woman is more confident that she will be believed and is less concerned that she will be penalized for dealing with a sexual harassment situation.

Employers and unions, including Bell Canada and its unions, the Canadian Telephone Employees Association (CTEA) and the Communications, Energy and Paper Workers Union of Canada (CEP), have recognized that sexual harassment harms everyone, as well as being counterproductive. Policies and processes for dealing with sexual harassment in the workplace are now widespread. But more importantly, it is recognized that as the composition of the labour force changes, new standards of behaviour are required of all employees. This means that activities which, in the past, may have been condoned (or even accepted) may in future be censured. A significant effort to redefine policies and practices is required, including communicating with and retraining all employees. The dynamics of the sexual harassment issue mean that male employees, especially those accustomed to traditional gender roles, have the largest part to play in this process of change.

As the country's largest telecommunications provider, Bell Canada employs some 50,000 Canadians, primarily in Ontario and Quebec. There is an enormous range of positions in the company including engineers, marketers, accountants, secretaries, computer programmers, telephone and equipment installers, equipment testers, network designers and maintenance people, operators, auto mechanics, sales people, clerical and technical support staff, as well as communications specialists, human resource specialists, trainers and auditors. The types of people who fill these part-time and full-time positions are nearly as diverse as the positions themselves: 51.4 percent are women; 7.9 percent belong to visible minorities; 2.1 percent are persons with disabilities; and 0.7 percent are of aboriginal origin. Approximately 75 percent of employees are represented by one of the two unions. Bell employees have an average of 14.6 years of service with the company and 27 percent of employees have completed education beyond high school.

Bell's historically large base of female employees, coupled with more recent efforts to transfer qualified women into traditionally male-dominated environments, has reinforced the need to ensure a work environment free from sexual harassment. In our competitive world, we know that more than moral imperatives are involved. It is critical that optimal employee/job matches be made, regardless of gender, ethnicity or disabilities. Today's best employee/job matches increasingly mean that previous gender roles must be discarded. All employees must be free to function at their fullest potential, which can happen only when the environment is free from harassment or discrimination.

Achieving a workplace free from harassment requires sustained efforts: we cannot expect employees to park their beliefs, attitudes and life experiences at the front door. These attributes make the people who they are, providing the creative spark employers require. They are also attributes which we, as employers, have helped to create over time through policy, practice and example. But the task is made easier when we all focus on clearly identifying what we mean by unacceptable behaviour, communicate this to all concerned and sanction inappropriate conduct. The strategies for change cannot be accomplished without working with the unions, who are key players in the lives of many employees. The following is a brief summary of the individual and collective efforts undertaken, or in progress, to achieve our objectives.

In the early 1980s, the company adopted a Human Rights Policy which covered harassment, entrenched it in its corporate practices and instituted a supporting human rights complaints process. Harassment is defined, in part, as "...behaviour which denies individuals their dignity and respect and which is offensive, embarrassing and humiliating." While harassment may exist on any of the grounds included in the *Canadian Human Rights Act*, the company focuses primarily on racial and sexual harassment. Sexual harassment is defined as behaviour of a sexual nature which meets the foregoing harassment conditions or which may be perceived as "...placing a condition of a sexual nature on employment or on any opportunity for training or promotion."

The harassment complaint process is outlined in the human rights policy document. Employees are encouraged to deal with harassment situations either directly or by approaching one of several alternate support persons such as a supervisor, union representative, or human rights counsellor. Emphasis is placed on providing employees with various options in order to make it easier for employees to deal with what for many is a highly stressful situation. Bell's overall approach in dealing with sexual harassment complaints is a non-punitive one, aimed at restoring wholeness to a previously unbalanced work situation. Local resolution of harassment situations is encouraged because it helps to strengthen the notion of personal responsibility for maintaining a harassment free workplace and helps to ensure that difficult situations are speedily resolved. Consistency across the organization is achieved by requiring that human rights counsellors be consulted in any situation where disciplinary or administrative action is contemplated.

In addition to the company's human rights policy, Bell and its unions many years ago negotiated a discrimination article in every collective agreement. This clause was updated in 1985 to include sexual harassment. Both unions have demonstrated their commitment to these articles by developing and implementing their own harassment awareness training for union representatives. In addition, both the CTEA and the CEP have actively supported company awareness and training initiatives. The CEP has also developed its own internal harassment policy as well as posters highlighting the need for union members to respect the dignity of co-workers.

The CTEA, CEP and the company recognize that endorsing and implementing a harassment policy is only a first step. Critical additional components to achieving success include educating managers and support staff about harassment issues, identifying potential solutions and, where necessary, redefining the boundaries of acceptable behaviour.

In the late 1980s, the company synthesized the harassment portion of its human rights policy and associated harassment complaints process into a harassment brochure which was distributed to all employees in 1990. The harassment brochure has also been provided to all district managers for posting in work areas. In addition, articles about sexual harassment regularly appear in company newsletters. A module on harassment was included in the Employment Equity Awareness Workshop, introduced in 1990, as well as in Industrial Relations Workshops.

In a cooperative vein, Bell, CTEA and CEP ensure that all women who enter the company's Qualifications Development Program (QDP), and their supervisors, attend a Sexual Harassment Awareness Workshop. The QDP is an employment equity special measure introduced several years ago to increase the representation of women in Trades, Technology and Operation (TTO) jobs. "QDPers" spend six months working in a selected trade or technology position in order to acquire the skills needed to qualify for the job when a permanent vacancy becomes available. The aim of the Sexual Harassment Awareness Workshop is to assist employees with the transition to a new work situation by reviewing company and union policies on harassment, explaining the harassment complaint process, and generally creating a supportive climate.

Another management/union collaborative initiative currently being developed is the release of a tripartite communiqué to all employees providing guidance on types of workplace "adornments" and personal paraphernalia which are inappropriate in a business environment. The tone and approach in the communiqué will be based, in part, on results of focus groups of both male and female employees scheduled to take place in 1994.

The company is also developing a harassment seminar which focuses on changes in our society and our company that are responsible for the increased awareness and recognition of sexual harassment. In the seminar, employees and supervisors are counselled that harassment must be dealt with seriously, swiftly and confidentially. Supervisors are also reminded that their duties include ensuring a work environment free from harassment.

As mentioned previously, Bell Canada, CTEA and CEP individually and collectively recognize sexual harassment as a serious issue affecting the workplace. Each is committed to a joint action plan which includes individual as well as long-term initiatives aimed at educating employees about the dynamics of gender politics inherent in sexual harassment, and at assisting employees to avoid harassing behaviour so as to provide all employees with a comfortable and productive work environment. These initiatives will be supplemented by others directed towards supervisors and staff until such time that sexual harassment is no longer an issue in the Bell Canada workplace.

Sexual Harassment at CN - A Clear Policy and Concrete Action

Marie Tellier

Marie Tellier is Assistant Vice-President, Employment Equity at Canadian National. Her responsibilities include developing and implementing programs, procedures and special measures to ensure the representation of target groups within the CN employee population.

CN's policy on sexual harassment is clear - we consider harassment to be unacceptable. All employees, regardless of their position, are entitled to a work environment free from harassment, be it physical or verbal. One form is just as harmful as the other. There is a distinction between direct harassment (unwelcome solicitations with a view to obtaining sexual favours, intimidation, unnecessary physical contact) and indirect harassment (sexual jokes, displaying objects or pictures of a sexual nature in the workplace, innuendoes or taunts about a person's body).

Sexual harassment is a problem that requires concrete action, and we have gone far beyond merely issuing a statement of good intentions. Before acting on the problem, however, we had first to admit that a problem existed and confront it. Talking openly about sexual harassment does not create or magnify the problem, just as ignoring it does not make it disappear. We decided to take a proactive approach to prevent all forms of harassment, in keeping with our

---

employment equity policies which promote, among other things, a work environment based on fairness and mutual respect.

Several factors led us to act promptly, for we realized the high cost of harassment: the problems and stress experienced by the victim, the cost of recruiting and training replacements for women who quit out of frustration, the cost of handling complaints, not to mention the negative impact on the Company's image.

The Company began to shape its sexual harassment policy in the mid-1980s, and took the first concrete steps in 1988. The entire process was guided by four main elements: confronting the situation, opening up frank discussions on the matter, developing tools to raise awareness about harassment, and implementing an effective mechanism to handle complaints.

A Two-faceted Approach

CN chose to raise awareness by developing and communicating a clear policy on sexual harassment, thereby eliminating, in large part, the problems caused by lack of information. First, there was an information campaign which included feature articles in the Company's newspaper, pamphlets and brochures distributed to all employees. These documents clearly outline CN's position on harassment, the types of behaviour that constitute sexual harassment, and the recourse available to victims of harassment.

Our main thrust, however, has focused on the second channel of communication: developing and setting up workshops for both management personnel and unionized employees. The purpose of these workshops is to introduce participants to the problem of sexual harassment, CN's policy on sexual harassment, and their roles and responsibilities in preventing and eliminating its occurrence. However, not everyone thought that awareness sessions were a good idea. Some thought that the sessions would be a waste of time; others thought they would create problems. Still others believed that harassment was caused by provocation, and that the awareness sessions would become the ideal forum for these people to talk about their point of view. Among those who supported the idea of awareness sessions were people who had experienced harassment and wanted to ask about their experiences.

The need to raise awareness was particularly important among:

1) those who were not aware that their behaviour constituted harassment;

2) the victims who were not aware of how to file a complaint and obtain the Company's support;

3) those who received the complaints but did not know how to handle them.

Organizing workshops seemed the most effective way of meeting the need to raise awareness. Workshops were preferred because they are an excellent communication method. They elicit frank and open discussion, allow the participants to share each others' perceptions, reconcile divergent points of view, and leave a lasting impression. The fact that the employer gives the matter such a high profile leads people to reflect on it and take it seriously.

Setting up the Workshops

Workshops are based on actual cases experienced by the Company and are led by human resources personnel who have been specially trained to deal with the issue. The facilitators are chosen on the basis of their experience and the empathy they have developed during their informal interventions in sexual harassment complaints.

To determine the effectiveness and relevance of the workshops, they were tested using two target groups, one representing management and one representing unionized employees, before being implemented across Canada. We carefully monitored reactions during the process of validation and measured the knowledge and skills acquired. Changes were then made to ensure the workshops fully met our needs.

Once delivery of the workshops was under way, the impact on participants was evaluated. The evaluations provided a wealth of information and confirmed the need for and effectiveness of the workshops.

The Workshops

The training modules for supervisors last two hours. A variety of teaching tools and techniques are used, including case studies, mini-docudramas on video, and acetates.

Since everyone comes to class with preconceived ideas about the subject, the first step is to define sexual harassment. The group discusses real life cases which help to identify unacceptable behaviour and to distinguish innocuous actions from downright offensive behaviour. They also learn how to deal with vague or unclear situations and how to differentiate between individual perceptions - behaviour that one woman finds offensive might be utterly trivial to another. Discussions are oriented to cover a wide range of possible scenarios.

The workshop then looks at the effects of harassment on the victim (poor performance, stress, denial of advancement opportunities) and on the workplace.

After explaining the roles and responsibilities of all parties in preventing harassment, the workshop then turns to the redress mechanism: procedures for filing a complaint, management investigation, and disciplinary action up to and including dismissal.

Procedures for handling complaints are explained in detail, focusing on how to interview the victim, how to conduct the investigation, and how to distinguish between a well-founded and unfounded complaint. Legislative requirements and the issue of the employer's liability are also discussed.

Training for Everyone at CN

The workshops were originally destined for managers and supervisors in order to deal with the immediate problem of handling complaints. The reactions from supervisors ran the gamut from total denial of the problem to recognition that it did in fact exist.

Once the supervisors were informed, the next step was raising awareness among the workers. Our research showed that close to 25 percent of our female employees were unaware of the procedure for filing a sexual harassment complaint. The workshop was therefore remodelled to address the needs of unionized employees, although its objectives are essentially the same as the workshop for management and supervisors.

Tangible Results

Most participants stated that they were better informed after this experience and felt more at ease talking about and dealing with the problem at work.

The results speak for themselves: the number of cases brought before the Canadian Human Rights Commission dropped drastically from 16 to four in just one year. On the other hand, the number of cases handled internally increased, as expected. When people are informed of their rights and available recourses, they feel more at ease filing a complaint because they know CN will listen and act upon it. The consequence is also good for CN because it enables us to be aware of problems and to deal with them quickly and effectively.

While we are fully aware that we can never eradicate harassment completely, we can still reduce its occurrence and diminish its negative effects. By increasing awareness and acceptance of individual rights, we are working to create an environment free of threats, humiliation and stress.

National Grocers' Workplace Harassment Policy

Roy Conliffe

Roy Conliffe has been with National Grocers Co. Ltd. since 1980. As Senior Vice-President of Human Resources and Industrial Relations, his responsibilities include human resources, industrial relations, safety, loss prevention, pension and benefits, family care and professional development programs.

National Grocers Co. Ltd. is the Ontario division of Loblaw Companies Limited. National Grocers, through its subsidiaries, operates a retail and wholesale food distribution organization in the province of Ontario with annual sales of over $3 billion.

National Grocers employs approximately 18,000 unionized employees in Ontario. It is the largest private sector employer of unionized employees in Ontario. All of the corporate stores and distribution centres and over 60 percent of the franchise operations are covered by collective agreements. Unions which are parties to these collective agreements include locals of the United Food and Commercial Workers International Union, the Retail, Wholesale and Department Store Union and the Teamsters.

Recognizing that our employees are vital to our success, National Grocers' Board of Directors developed a number of operating principles and policies which define the way our employees should be treated. One of these is the Workplace Harassment Policy. The policy is divided into three sections.

A.   Definitions

National Grocers recognizes the diverse and multicultural composition of its work force and also appreciates the dignity and worth of each member. We provide equal rights and opportunities for all without discrimination. Every employee has the right to work in an environment free from harassment due to sex, colour, racial origin, creed, marital status, disability, age, ancestry, place of origin, ethnic origin, citizenship, record of offences, or family status. No such harassment will be tolerated.

Particular attention is drawn to sexual harassment which is any conduct, comment, gesture or contact of a sexual nature that is likely to cause offence or humiliation to an employee or that might, on reasonable grounds, be perceived by that employee as placing a condition or a sexual nature on employment or career development. Sexual harassment will be considered to have taken place if a reasonable person ought to have known that such behaviour was unwelcome.

B.   Responsibilities and Penalties

Harassment of any form is a serious offence subject to a wide range of disciplinary sanctions up to and including discharge. Some situations may be serious enough to constitute a criminal offence. All employees are responsible for ensuring that the workplace is free from harassment. Upon becoming aware that some form of harassment is occurring, managers are responsible for taking corrective action, in consultation with Human Resources or Industrial Relations, even if no formal complaint is made. The Ontario Human Rights Code states that a person who has authority to prevent or discourage harassment may be held responsible for failing to do so.

C.   Complaints

An employee experiencing harassment should immediately request that the harasser cease the offensive behaviour. Employees should keep a written record of dates, times, specific behaviour and witnesses. The incident(s) should be reported promptly to the appropriate Human Resources/ Industrial Relations Manager. The Human Resources/Industrial Relations Manager will prepare a report which will be shown to the complainant, the alleged harasser and Legal Counsel. Identities will not be otherwise revealed unless necessary for fact finding. All material will be kept under confidential cover and separate from employee records.

If the complaint is substantiated, Human Resources/Industrial Relations will advise the harasser's supervisor, the head of the division and Legal Counsel. The range of possible disciplinary measures varies from providing a formal apology to dismissal. Where a complaint is not upheld, the complainant may appeal to the head of the division. These actions do not supersede complaint procedures established by legislation or by a collective agreement.

The Workplace Harassment Policy applies to all employees within National Grocers Co. Ltd. More specifically, the policy will apply to all full-time and part-time salaried and unionized employees of Fortinos, Freshmart, Hasty Market, IPCF, Loblaws Supermarkets Limited, Mr. Grocer, National Grocers Co. Ltd., Valu-Mart, Your Independent Grocer, and Zehrs.

To date, National Grocers' senior management board and representatives from each of the union locals previously noted, have reviewed and approved the Workplace Harassment Policy. The next step, currently being explored, is how best to communicate the policy to all company employees. Posters clearly stating the policy will be distributed to all company locations for posting. Every employee will also receive a package which will include the policy itself, a list of frequently asked questions and their appropriate answers, and a full explanation of the various steps in the complaint process. A comprehensive article regarding the policy may also be placed in various company newsletters and publications.

These three steps will make the policy language available to employees. However, it is felt that a more active and personal approach is also required, to better emphasize the importance of the policy and the fact that "all employees are responsible for ensuring that the workplace is free from harassment." To this end, Human Resources and Industrial Relations representatives will work together with middle management to communicate the policy to employees. It is hoped that the inclusion of middle management in the communication process will make the policy's language come alive for all employees and encourage them to participate in establishing and maintaining the policy in their workplace.

A presentation is being considered for salaried employees in groups of 25 to 30 people per session. Time will then be made available for questions and discussion. A clear understanding of the company's definition of harassment and complaint process is crucial to the policy's effectiveness within the work environment. Equally important is each employee's acceptance of personal responsibility in putting the policy into place. For these reasons, the opportunity for discussion amongst employees is felt to be extremely valuable in that it will enable individuals to ask questions, express concerns and clarify their understanding of the policy and their role in ensuring that their workplace is free from harassment for both themselves and their co-workers.

This same presentation format is being considered for the company's warehouse supervisors and store managers. If this takes place, it is hoped that these individuals will take on the responsibility of making a similar presentation on the policy to their employees. Warehouse supervisors will be asked to present and discuss the policy with their unionized warehouse employees and drivers. Store managers will be asked to make the presentation to their store's department managers, who in turn will present and discuss the policy with the employees working in each of their departments.

This type of filtering communication strategy is currently seen as beneficial for three reasons:

(1) In taking on the responsibility of introducing and explaining the policy to others, it is hoped that the "presenters" will take on a sense of ownership for the policy and its message. This sense of ownership will translate into a strong show of support for the policy, thereby adding credibility and weight to the policy in their employees' eyes.

(2) The policy's message may have a greater impact on employees if it is made known to them by their immediate supervisor with whom they work on a regular basis.

(3) Should a situation concerning harassment occur, the employee(s) involved may feel more comfortable about reporting the incident if he or she has already been assured that his or her immediate supervisor supports the policy.

National Grocers' Workplace Harassment Policy will also be presented and discussed as part of the company's upcoming Diversity Management program. This program, which was developed by Human Resources, will focus on:

(1) Creating a link between diversity management, equity and National Grocers' strategic vision and operating principles.

(2) Updating opinion leaders on the existing external and internal status of equity at National Grocers with respect to demographics, legislation, etc.

(3) Communicating relevant initiatives of National Grocers' Employment Equity plan.

(4) Identifying managers' and employees' responsibilities in creating an equitable employment system at National Grocers.

Part of the employment equity segment of this program will address discrimination in the workplace. As harassment can often be a direct result of discriminatory attitudes and/or actions, the discussion generated by the topic of discrimination will then lead into the existence of the company's Workplace Harassment Policy. At this point in the program, the Workplace Harassment Policy will be presented and reviewed in full. Various hypothetical cases of harassment will also be introduced, in order to encourage open and comprehensive discussion around the policy.

The Diversity Management program has received final approval and will soon be presented to all employees. Human Resources representatives will be presenting the program to vice-presidents, directors, managers, and finally, all company employees.

Consequently, National Grocers' Workplace Harassment Policy will be presented and reviewed with all company employees twice, in order to ensure a full awareness and understanding of the policy throughout the entire company.

National Grocers Co. Ltd. employs approximately 20,000 salaried and unionized employees. The process of educating this considerable number of individuals about our Workplace Harassment Policy has now begun and will continue indefinitely in order to ensure that all of our employees are assured of a workplace that is open, comfortable, and free of harassment.

Sexual Harassment Policies in Canada's Banks: Eliminating Harassment Through Cultural Change

Helen Sinclair

Helen Sinclair has been President of the Canadian Bankers Association since 1989, prior to which she held several senior executive positions with the Bank of Nova Scotia.

As federally regulated institutions, Canada's banks are obliged to abide by the provisions of the *Canada Labour Code* and the *Canadian Human Rights Act*. It should therefore come as no surprise that the banks are in full compliance with regulations regarding harassment of all kinds, including sexual harassment. As required, these policies are posted in all bank workplaces; they define sexual harassment, cover complaint and investigative procedures and disciplinary measures, and guarantee confidentiality of the complainant. Those are the legal obligations, and bank compliance is not an issue.

What is much more significant is that all of the six major domestic banks have gone to considerable lengths to address the spirit as well as the letter of the law. No matter how clear, comprehensive and impressive the policy, decent behaviour cannot be legislated -- it arises from attitude and culture. This became particularly clear in the banks' experience with employment equity: since the early 1970s, a number of the banks have had policies indicating a commitment to equal employment opportunities. Yet in the 1980s, when the banks began to actively measure progress towards employment equity goals, it became clear that the existence of a non-discriminatory policy had been insufficient to ensure an equitable workplace. Systemic discriminatory barriers ingrained in the culture had impeded the progress of women.

Bank management began to realize that the culture had to change - not just to permit banks to live up to their legal and moral obligations, but also to achieve the business benefits of a fair, equitable, diverse workplace where every individual is able to live up to his or her own potential and where productivity is inevitably enhanced.

Sexual harassment is clearly a discriminatory barrier in employment. While we do not know whether sexual harassment was a particularly pervasive problem at the banks in the past, the potential for abuse and coercion was certainly there - and the prevailing culture in society as well as in the banks did not adequately recognize this potential.

Within the broader context of creating a fair and equitable workplace, the banks have zeroed in on eliminating harassment and have recognized the importance of creating a culture - through training, education and awareness - where sexual harassment, quite simply, is not tolerated. Posting and enforcing anti-harassment policies is not sufficient; they must be institutionalized.

Institutionalization starts with awareness, and awareness starts at day one. All the banks make sure that new employees are informed of anti-harassment policies. At the Bank of Montreal, for example, entry level training programs include a fully developed component on harassment. In training and education programs throughout the banking system, awareness and understanding are the critical elements. It is not enough for employees to know their bank has an anti-harassment policy. Training is focused on explaining the reasons for the policies - why harassment is wrong and how destructive it is to a healthy workplace environment.

Ongoing communications - through employee publications, brochures, seminars and presentations and, in the case of Bank of Nova Scotia, a specially produced video - are designed to reinforce the climate of awareness and understanding.

Efforts to institutionalize the elimination of harassment have been extended in recent years by making management of harassment issues a direct responsibility of every manager and supervisor - not just of human resource officers and senior executives. By making everyone in a position of authority accountable, the banks increase awareness and enforcement. Achieving a harassment-free workplace is becoming part of the job of today's banker in this country.

With these changes, we believe attitudes have begun to change in a meaningful way. And the advances that women have made in bank management during the past decade have undoubtedly helped sensitize the institutions to the issue.

This is not to suggest that there has been no resistance. Cultural change inevitably means uncertainty, and there were some fears at the banks that increased focus on the issue and vastly simplified complaint procedures would foster an environment where people lodged false complaints for vindictive purposes. This has not happened; all complaints are thoroughly investigated, and we have seen little indication of frivolous accusations.

All of the banks are committed to treating complaints seriously - and to making their commitment well known and understood throughout the workplace. Offences are not swept under the rug. At Toronto Dominion Bank, for instance, the reprimand will vary depending on the nature of the offence, but it could include suspension without pay for three days or termination from the bank. In cases where an offender remains in his or her position, the reprimand will include the offender's agreement to hold a staff meeting of the branch or business unit and explain the nature of the offence and why such behaviour is unacceptable. In this way the treatment is highly visible, and all colleagues in the workplace can see that the bank pays much more than lip service to its policies.

It would be premature to suggest that sexual harassment has been eliminated from the Canadian banking workplace. With tens of thousands of men and women working together in thousands of different locations across Canada and around the world, the potential for harassment may always exist. But the banks have set elimination as a clear-cut goal, and for several years they have been making a concerted effort to effect the necessary cultural change. We believe the banks have shown considerable leadership in this respect and that they are on the right course. We do, indeed, "get it" - and we are going to get rid of it.

Sexual Harassment in the Construction Industry

Jo-Anne Stead

Jo-Anne Stead was the Coordinator of the Canadian Construction Association's employment equity program from its inception in 1988 until 1993. Prior to that she worked in the private sector consulting unit of the Ontario Women's Directorate, assisting employers and associations with voluntary employment equity programs.

Sexual harassment is probably not a major topic of conversation around the lunch table at your average construction site. With the construction industry stereotypically recognized as one of the last bastions of male-dominated employment, it is generally thought that sexual harassment would not be a big concern. Times are changing, however, and as women are slowly making inroads onto the construction worksite in the trades, technologies, and professions, this important workplace issue is being dealt with in a more active manner.

The representation of women in the construction industry has been gradually increasing over the last 20 years. While it is very common to find women in the administrative occupations, it is much more unusual to find them working in the trades and even in some of the professions such as engineering and architecture. Initiatives have been conducted over the last two decades to address the disparities in the number of women and men working in construction. For instance, the Canadian Construction Association had a full-time Employment Equity Program from 1988 to 1993 to try to increase the

---

representation of women and other designated group members in the industry and to educate the construction industry as to what they can do to make the workplace a more equitable one.

Although such changes take time, some results are evident. The percentage of women working in the construction trades has increased from 1.3 percent in 1980 (representing 8,000 women) to 2.4 percent (representing 17,000 women) in 1990. With the number of women in the construction industry so low, employers once thought that sexual harassment was not an issue that needed to be addressed. With more women now in the industry, and with the increased awareness of sexual harassment and its harmful affects on the work force, more employers, and the industry in general, are starting to respond.

Early female recruits in the construction trades faced an intimidating work environment. In far too many cases, harassment based on gender destroyed the aspirations of women in search of challenging careers. As John Halliwell, a former president of the Canadian Construction Association (CCA), observed:

> In the early 1990s, the scene is changing as construction employers realize the value of a safe work environment, free of harassment, where women are truly colleagues. The attitudes of male construction workers are also changing as we witness a much greater acceptance of women in non-traditional occupations.

The construction industry is unique for many reasons, not just because the work force is predominately male. The physical nature of the work, the outdoor environment, working in a team, and the variety of jobs available make the industry unique. Construction employs about 700,000 people across the country, and approximately 50 percent of the construction labour force is unionized.

Trying to determine the extent to which sexual harassment occurs in the industry is diffcult. Most of the women working in the industry today are singled out because they are the only women on the site and have to deal with the isolation, the stress of being a pioneer in their field and break new ground with their male colleagues. In such an environment it would be remarkable if sexual harassment didn't occur on some sites. After talking with many women who have worked in construction over the years, it appears there is no generalization that can be used to describe the amount of harassment experienced on the worksite. Some women say they've had no problems with sexual harassment at all, while others report terrible experiences that eventually led them to quit the industry.

An example of one woman's experiences is found in the extensive research project conducted by Sharon Goldberg for the Amalgamated Construction Association (ACA) of B.C. The report, Women in Construction, funded by Employment and Immigration Canada, contains tradeswomen's comments on topics such as sexual harassment. Here is what one woman says:

> The reason women leave the trades is that they start out all gung ho for a wonderful career, something they really enjoy doing, and after four years of apprenticeship and sticking it out and putting up with it.... If they can put up with it to get their TQ ticket, a lot of them might make it further than that. But I think a lot of them drop out because of the harassment, the verbal harassment, the posters, pin-ups, scrawls on the bathroom walls with your name on it, it's never ending. And it doesn't matter what job you're on, who you work for, the guys you're working with, you're always going to find someone who's going to do something.

Although this is only one woman's experience and definitely does not represent every woman's viewpoint, it describes how some women working in the trades find that harassment is a problem. It is evident that harassment exists in many different forms in the construction industry, as in other industries. It varies from the extreme of assault to the blatant and obvious verbal harassment in the forms of name calling, jokes, propositions, to leers and hand gestures, and to the passive, yet still damaging, pin-ups and posters of nude and semi-nude women.

With many worksites receiving women for the first time, sexual harassment is just becoming an issue to many construction companies and their associations. Construction associations are beginning to learn more about sexual harassment and what they can do to help.

CCA has published a sample sexual harassment policy for employers in its Employment Equity Guide and has a file on various policies and case histories in its employment equity program library.

Other associations, such as the Amalgamated Construction Association in Vancouver, are also taking action. The Association's report on Women in Construction included a recommendation on sexual harassment: "That policies and practices on gender harassment and sexual harassment be adopted by A.C.A. and promoted to the membership and the industry." Allan Bennett, past President of A.C.A., said his board of directors fully endorsed this recommendation (along with the nine others in the report) and planned to implement it. Bennett said the association will also be applying to the provincial government for funding to produce an educational pamphlet on sexual harassment in the workplace that could be distributed to its members.

Some other organizations have been taking a proactive approach to educating their members about sexual harassment. For instance, the Terrazzo, Tile and Marble Association, and the Terrazzo, Tile and Marble Guild, along with the Canadian Construction Association's Employment Equity Program co-sponsored, in May 1992, a one-day workshop on Harassment in the Workplace. The workshop covered such issues as: the faces of harassment, understanding harassment, acting against harassment, and harassment prevention. The seminar gave the employers and union representatives a greater understanding of the background of sexual harassment, the legal implications arising from the Ontario and Canadian human rights legislation and some examples of real-life situations. Many of those in attendance weren't aware of what sexual harassment meant in a legal sense, and appreciated being informed of all the items covered in the human rights codes.

With approximately half of the construction work force being unionized in Canada, unions also have a responsibility for educating their members about this important issue.

Some work is already being done. For instance, the Provincial Building and Construction Trades Council, the Ontario Women's Directorate and the Ministry of Skills Development in Ontario have jointly sponsored the development of a training module to address equity in apprenticeship. The training covers such topics as work force diversity, employment equity, and harassment in the workplace. It is aimed at apprentices as well as union instructors.

The ultimate responsibility for a greater understanding of sexual harassment, however, lies with the employer. It is the employer's responsibility to ensure that policies are in place to address harassment and that there is recourse if employees report incidents of harassment.

Some of the larger construction companies that have women working in the trades are taking the lead and are taking steps to address the workplace issue of sexual harassment.

Eastern Construction Company Limited, one of the five largest general contractors in Canada, which has done work from Halifax to Vancouver, wrote and implemented in early 1992 a code of conduct dealing with harassment in the workplace. Kerry MacDonald, Eastern's Vice-President of Field Operations, said they decided they needed to take a more proactive approach towards this issue. They realized that religious and sexual harassment was a workplace issue. "I started it up myself," said MacDonald. "I've personally run into religious and sexual harassment and realized that people aren't very sensitive to this." The policy was written primarily for the field operations and addresses all forms of harassment, including the issue of pin-ups. MacDonald said the policy was reviewed and approved by the Ontario Human Rights Commission.

Eastern's two-page harassment policy includes a definition of what harassment is: "Sexual harassment is any unwanted attention of a sexual nature such as remarks about appearance or personal life, offensive written or visual actions such as graffiti, jokes or degrading pictures and pin-ups, physical contact of any kind and sexual demands." The policy goes on to outline the steps anyone being harassed should take and states that all incidents of harassment will be thoroughly and promptly investigated. Disciplinary action will be taken when complaints are sustained and this could include suspension or dismissal.

Although Eastern Construction is a leader in the field to date with their policy, there are signs that other companies are following suit. For instance, PCL Construction Ltd. says it plans to write and implement a harassment policy this year. The larger general contractors are not the only ones that are becoming more proactive. Some of the smaller construction companies are interested in developing harassment policies.

David Simms, area manager of Schurman Construction in Prince Edward Island, says that management in his company wants to put together a harassment policy. They realize that it does happen and they want to be prepared.

It is an encouraging sign that construction companies, associations and unions are becoming more aware of, and more active in addressing, this serious workplace issue.

If You Don't "Get It," You Can't Stop It

Etta Wharton

Etta Wharton has been responsible for affirmative action and employment equity programs at Ontario Hydro since 1984. She is currently Director of its Employment Equity Division, a position she has held since 1991.

Companies and other institutions across Canada are writing sexual harassment policies. Some are motivated by fear of legal and/or public exposure and some by prudence. A smaller number have a generalized, if not well-articulated, view that it's the right thing to do. Fewer still are those that understand that stopping sexual harassment is inextricably intertwined with achieving equality for women in the work force. Although there is plenty of rhetoric about the economic costs of inequality, there seems to be little evidence of an acceptance by business leaders that investing in ending harassment and achieving equality produce immediate improvements in effectiveness and productivity. Otherwise such investments would be more widespread.

Some of these policies will take years to write and approve. Such a long time-frame for the formulation of policy, whether public, institutional or even personal, implies a lack of understanding, a lack of consensus, or ambivalence or disagreement about what, if anything, needs to be done.

Sexual harassment is against the law in Canada. Nevertheless, there will be lengthy debate among the policy writers and even more among the decision-makers, managers and employees to whom such policies apply, as to what sexual harassment really is.

There will be denials that sexual harassment occurs in such a "fine company as ours" and statements that a few trouble-makers are "blowing it up out of all proportion." The calls to remember that men are also harassed by women may exceed the number of such incidents likely to occur in a decade, and the issue of same sex harassment may prove too uncomfortable for any discussion at all. Concerns about malicious complaints and the protection of the rights of the accused will be exaggerated. A need will be felt to define the degree of responsibility women have for their own harassment. Attempts to address the abusive or poisoned work environment will provoke discussion about freedom of speech, women lacking a sense of humour, male bonding and the appropriate length of skirts.

Relatively little discussion about the pain or the consequences to the victim will occur at the rarefied levels of senior decision making, and almost never will those discussions be held with actual victims of sexual harassment. Because the issue is so fraught with feeling, so emotional and so visceral, discussion by senior decision makers will be kept out of the realms of such messy things as people's feelings, their pain, their losses and their hope for justice. It will be organizational talk, clean and without passion, virtually aseptic, about processes, structures, numbers, checks and balances, and reporting mechanisms.

Why is it so difficult to deal with something that is illegal and so obviously damaging to women? Why are complications continually being thrown into the processes of understanding and dealing with sexual harassment?

The answer is complex, of course, but stating that truism is of no great help. One simple but major reason is that a great many people do not think that sexual harassment is wrong, despite the fact it is illegal. There is an attitude that sexual harassment may not be nice in polite company, but surely it is not "wrong" enough to be against the law or "bad" enough for a man to be fired! This prevents the self-censoring of behaviour that is essential to preventing wrongful actions.

Theft is also against the law. As a society we have more consensus and less difficulty in dealing with thieves than with sexual harassers. That is because most people think that it is wrong to steal, censor their own actions accordingly, and expect others and the justice system to do so as well. Even among the small proportion of the population that steals, it is likely that most recognize that their actions are wrong. They may be willing to take the risk of trying to get away with it, but rarely is it argued that there is nothing wrong with taking the property of others or that it was only done in jest.

The apparent incomprehension regarding sexual harassment extends beyond the intellectual, because for almost all men, understanding that sexual harassment is wrong (or, to use the vernacular "getting it") means empathy for feelings they will never experience personally. And empathy for "the other" seems to be very difficult to generate.

Efforts to eliminate sexual harassment in the workplace are also impeded by the many still unresolved gender issues in our society of which our workplaces are microcosms. Role stereotyping, misogyny, inability to listen to the voice of "the other," differences in power, both structural and personal, and the view that the structures of the *status quo* have no gender are all still getting in the way.

As well, true understanding of sexual harassment and the systems that support it means rolling out the dreaded f-word ("feminist"!), and there are few things more deeply in the closet in Canadian corporations than feminist viewpoints and analysis.

The way may seem bleak but it is not impassable. This is a case where the journey becomes the destination. Imperfect though they may be, sexual harassment policies must be developed and put in place. Imperfect though the process will be in operation, there must be an expectation that some action will be taken. Ending sexual harassment in a large institution is dependent upon the actions of hundreds if not thousands of individuals. They will not all be unified in either their under-standing or commitment, but the corporate expectations for standards of behaviour need to be clearly articulated. In ending sexual harassment, cognitive dissonance can be on the side of the change makers.

Organizations need to take a stand. It is wonderful when the CEO and the executive group recognize the problem of sexual harassment. But if one or more of them doesn't "get it," they should trust those in the organization who do. This may mean learning to listen to women and acting on women's experience of reality even when it is not shared by the decision-making group.

Where an organization starts, in both its understanding and its assessment of the problem, is not where it will end up. If the issue is dealt with seriously and the policy is not just cosmetic, there will be learning and deepening of understanding and increased effectiveness.

Ontario Hydro's first sexual harassment policy was established in 1982. It has been revised twice since and reviewed again in 1993. The changes each time have not been to correct false starts but to incorporate this increased understanding to address such issues as poisoned work environment, the proactive role of supervisors in managing harassment and the role of third parties who are aware of harassment. To deal effectively with harassment we recognize that we must continuously re-examine and improve policies, procedures, education and communication.

But even the perfect policy - were such a document to exist - would be useless without the will to label the problem and to act. Instilling the will to label and to act in supervisors, managers, employees and employee representatives is the ongoing challenge.

Education, communication, and defining expected standards of behaviour all help, as do peer pressure, sanctions and public exposure, painful though these may be.

There are really significant differences in the attitude and effectiveness of Ontario Hydro in dealing with sexual harassment today, as compared with the early 1980s. The increased understanding is occurring on several levels: recognition that sexual harassment is wrong, that it is bad for productive work and costly to the company, and that it inhibits our goal of gender equality.

There is a significant increase in the number of reported cases of sexual harassment. This apparent contradiction is not a real one. An increase in reported cases indicates that more women are willing to come forward and thus believe they will get support and action. These are signs of an effective program although, as in cases of sexual assault, reported cases are probably still only a fraction of the total actually occurring.

More supervisors are taking action to rid the workplace of sexually offensive material. More supervisors are believing women and are personally separating themselves from collusive peer behaviour and attitudes. Unions are taking a stronger official position with respect to harassment including, in a few cases, refusing to launch grievances against disciplinary actions. The unions have indicated that they are prepared to sanction union officials who act inappropriately.

Most sexual harassment complaints which have been investigated have been substantiated. In a few cases they have not been, for lack of witnesses. There appears to be no evidence of malicious complaints.

But while progress has been made, obstacles remain. In the first place, an organization of almost 29,000 individuals will not have uniform beliefs on any issue, especially not on one as closely connected to personal values as sexual harassment. Second, the response of supervisors has not always been adequate, whether due to a fundamental lack of understanding, lack of empathy, or an unwillingness to face the issue. At the supervisory level there can still be denial or trivialization of the problem of sexual harassment and a desire to restrict the definition to cases of sexual assault or coercive harassment.

Some supervisors will only react, that is, in response to a specific complaint but not the general working environment. Some will act to contain the problem of sexual harassment rather than confront it directly.

Collusion among co-workers, employees and supervisors, or supervisors and union stewards still occurs. Collusion must be seen as encompassing more than active complicity. Silence and denial in the face of acts of sexual harassment or a poisoned work environment also amount to collusion.

In some cases, complainants get inadequate emotional support whether from management or unions. Many women are reluctant to report incidents of harassment because they fear reprisal, not only by the harasser but by co-workers and "the system." Many are still concerned that making a complaint of harassment will label them as troublemakers and limit their career opportunities.

This stigma can be so stressful, especially when co-workers actively support the harasser and ostracize the victim, that in some cases, even when the harassment has been substantiated and the harasser disciplined, the victim has requested transfer to another work unit.

Occasionally, the victim still is portrayed as the problem. For example, suddenly concerns are raised about the victim's performance, as if this somehow excused the harassment. This was a significant problem in the early days of efforts to deal with sexual harassment but it has now largely, though not entirely, disappeared.

Just as an individual must make the effort through hard introspection and reflection, to change from being a person who overlooks sexual harassment to being a person who "gets it" and will take a stand on it, so must an organization.

This process includes recognizing one's own warts and weaknesses and underlies our desire to be very open and honest about the issue and our progress. Organizational behaviour must model expected personal behaviour. Scrutiny by employees of any gaps or hypocrisy is hard and relentless.

Our journey continues.

Section V

The Labour Movement's
Perspectives and Initiatives

Creating Harassment-Free Zones

Nancy Riche

---

*Nancy Riche is Executive Vice-President of the
Canadian Labour Congress with responsibility for
Women and Human Rights. She is also Vice-President
of the International Confederation of Free Trade Unions,
responsible for international women's issues.*

I think back to the mid-1970s when I was a trade union activist
in Newfoundland. We had invited Constance Backhouse to
speak to an International Women's Day forum. Only about
10 people showed up. I remember sending a questionnaire about
sexual harassment to our members (14,000) and we had three
replies (two were jokes). I remember talking to women who
had been sexually harassed in their workplace and who wouldn't
let me talk to anyone else about their situation. I remember
working for months with CBC in St. John's on a show on sexual
harassment. It was never broadcast because all the women I
spoke to (maybe 10) would not, could not, speak on the issue
publicly.

I know that my experience in those days was not an isolated
one. Untold numbers of women across the country agonized
in private, suffered profound damage to their emotional and
physical health, left or were fired from their jobs, and lost
their families.

Less than 20 years have passed and, while harassment certainly continues to plague the workplace, I believe we are making tremendous progress toward eliminating it. The key to this progress has been, and continues to be, the raising of women's voices, the breaking of the silence. Each courageous woman who brought her story forward, who fought the system despite the personal and financial costs involved, has made it easier for others of us to speak up and has helped strengthen the collective force of women as we have organized for equality and against harassment over these years. And without question, it is the individual and collective strength of women which has given the problem of sexual harassment the priority it has today.

And sexual harassment is an issue of top priority - for women workers, for the women's movement, for the labour movement.

The Canadian Labour Congress passed its first resolution to fight sexual harassment in 1980. Women spoke powerfully on the convention floor of the pain and humiliation caused by sexual harassment. And men spoke too. While it passed easily, I cannot honestly say that all delegates accorded this resolution the serious attention it deserved. This is not true today. At the 1992 CLC convention, a priority policy statement, "We Can Do It: End Violence Against Women," which included a policy against sexual harassment, was passed unanimously. Delegates were riveted during the floor debate. If there were those who were unsympathetic, they knew better than to show their feelings in this gathering, by word, by gesture or even by obvious indifference.

Such a profound change is reflective of the gains made over the years and of the increasing determination of the union movement to achieve equality for women, inside our movement as well as within the workplace and society. It reflects a growing understanding of the seriousness of harassment and of the extent to which it undermines basic union principles of solidarity and human rights. It is reflective of vocal, well-organized and militant union activists, mostly women, who simply will not tolerate harassment any more.

Through this process, we are learning not only how to better fight sexual harassment, but also to recognize that sexual harassment is part of an ugly spectrum of violence against women. It is an integral aspect of a structure of unequal relations between men and women, made more intense by an economic and social system which reserves wealth, privilege and power for a small, male elite. It imposes roles, stereotypes and behaviours which confine and oppress women.

The harassment women encounter is not limited to sexual harassment. Visible minority women, aboriginal women, lesbians, and women with disabilities are subjected every day to prejudiced actions, words and attitudes which cannot easily be separated from the oppression which they experience as women.

Many unions identified sexual, racial and personal harassment as issues many years ago, but we are now realizing that resolutions, policies and contract language are not enough in themselves to combat the problem.

We are making the progress we must make on a number of fronts. Our ability to fight harassment has been enhanced by a steadily evolving jurisprudence through arbitation, from the courts and human rights tribunals.

But much remains to be done by and in our movement; we cannot rely on jurisprudence and legal procedures alone. Complaints taken forward, as we all know, can take years to resolve, taxing the health, economic survival and energy of the survivors. The complaints process is only an individual solution to a collective problem.

We are working hard to obtain fast, accessible and safe redress procedures. For example, a recent policy agreed to by Toronto Hydro and CUPE Local 1 allows workers making claims of harassment to leave the workplace, with pay, until an investigation has been made. Unions are re-examining bargaining language for enhanced effectiveness.

Within our own ranks, we are establishing clear policies and procedures to ensure workers' rights during union events. Increasingly, we are educating and sensitizing stewards, other union leaders and the rank and file so that individuals who suffer sexual harassment can approach their union with confidence. We are encouraging workers themselves to take responsibility for ensuring that harassment of co-workers is not tolerated and is eliminated from the workplace.

This last aspect is extremely important in fighting harassment and inequality. As CLC policy puts it, "all brothers and sisters in the labour movement (must) become actively involved in these issues, individually and collectively, by taking positive steps on a daily basis to change society. This can include such measures as: objecting to sexist and racist or homophobic jokes; playing equal roles in parenting and household responsibilities; boycotting stores that sell pornographic magazines or videos. Men have a particular responsibility in this regard to take charge of their own behaviour, to treat these issues seriously...." A daily, individual commitment to working for equality is essential if our collective goals of social and economic justice are ever to be achieved - because the personal *is* political.

Sexual Harassment: A Comprehensive Approach

James McCambly

James McCambly *is the founding President of the Canadian Federation of Labour, a post he has held since 1982. Prior to that he was the Executive-Secretary of the Canadian office of the Building and Construction Trades Department, AFL-CIO.*

Unions historically have protected workers where laws affecting the workplace do not exist, are poorly enforced, or are compromised. Unions have been, and will continue to be, advocates for victims of all types of workplace abuse. The protection of workers from sexual harassment by persons holding supervisory positions and by co-workers is an important service provided by unions. Sexual harassment can damage an employee's physical, psychological and economic well-being. It is a demoralizing, counterproductive abuse of power which reduces the equality of those affected and ultimately results in losses of productivity, workplace efficiency, and valuable employees.

Sexual harassment is any form of unwelcome, unsolicited or unwarranted behaviour that is sexual in nature, such as repeated comments about physical appearance or sexual activity, and includes unwanted touching. While sexual harassment itself can take the form of a straightforward demand for sexual compliance by a person in a position of authority, it can also be identified in its more subtle form as taking place if the behaviour of a person in a supervisory role, or a colleague, creates a "poisoned" environment through demeaning or derogatory behaviour or speech. The Canadian Federation of Labour welcomes the broadening of the legal understanding of the psychological effects of sexual harassment which sees it occurring even if there are no economic consequences to the victim, such as a loss of one's job or a loss of seniority.

Addressing sexual harassment with specific measures is not new for labour. There are many examples of unions developing tough harassment policies and procedures long before sexual harassment itself was addressed by laws.

The unions affiliated to the Canadian Federation of Labour offer workers a variety of mechanisms as a redress to sexual harassment. If the claim of harassment is directed at a supervisor, the grievance procedure is the most often used service provided to workers. The grievance procedure involves a careful, unbiased, transparent, investigatory process that also protects the confidentiality of the files of the complainant and the accused. Another option is to negotiate specific clauses in collective agreements in order to clearly define the method of redress. Through a shop steward, who is usually on site, unions provide fast, safe contact and assistance. Union officers are also available to assist the worker in complaining to federal or provincial human rights commissions. While unions offer general counselling services to members, many now have or are in the process of establishing specialized sexual harassment counselling programs as well as educational and advocacy services. The Education Department of the Canadian Federation of Labour has developed a seminar entitled, "Sexual Harassment; It's No Joke."

There are occasions when a union is called upon by co-workers who are the complainant and the accused person. Counselling is formally and informally offered to both parties involved in the case of co-worker harassment, and the opportunity to resolve the problem is also given. However, the employee experiencing harassment has, in all situations, the individual right to refuse this form of resolution. Some unions have policies and procedures which also apply internally. One union affiliated to the Canadian Federation of Labour, for example, has a tough policy dealing with sexual harassment by employers that also applies to co-workers. This union's procedure involves a process whereby a complainant can request that the head office directly investigate the situation.

While unions undertake every action they can, it is incumbent on employers, as the sole holder of power and authority in the workplace, to provide a healthy working environment. That includes protecting workers from harassment. Employers are in the best position to introduce changes and perhaps in most need of changing their behaviour - two-thirds of the reported cases of sexual harassment at the workplace involve managers and subordinates. Sexual harassment can increase employee turnover and be costly in terms of efficiency. It can also result in civil litigation, increased workers' compensation assessments, broad remedial initiatives imposed by human rights tribunals, and awards for loss of wages by human rights commissions.

The first step in developing an effective sexual harassment policy in the workplace is coordination between the union and the employer. Even in non-unionized workplaces, credible efforts must be undertaken by management to work with employees. Employers must make it clear that sexual harassment is illegal and will not be tolerated. Employees must be given a firm, clear process for dealing with complaints. It is also important to stress that complaints will be dealt with in strict confidentiality and that credible consequences have been established. Finally, counselling and education awareness programs will increase the effectiveness of policies against sexual harassment.

Sexual harassment is a form of discriminatory behaviour that the Canadian Federation of Labour is committed to eradicating. All people should be treated with dignity and respect by employers and co-workers.

As a national central labour body representing 14 affiliated unions, the Canadian Federation of Labour strongly endorses those policies and procedures that reflect zero tolerance for sexual harassment and, by extension, zero tolerance for any form of discrimination directed at any worker in any workplace.

The CNTU's Policies on Sexual Harassment

Marie Pepin

Marie Pepin was Coordinator of the Status of Women Division of the Confederation of National Trade Unions (CNTU) for 1992-93 and, since 1990, has been a member of the National Committee for the Status of Women of the CNTU.

A Definition

Sexual harassment has only recently been recognized as such. In the 1970s, women finally put a name to the behaviour with sexual overtones that they were being subjected to at work. While very unpleasant and at times dangerous to the health of some women, such behaviour was customary. In fact, in some workplaces - the hotel and restaurant industries, for example - it was considered one of the risks that came with the job, and this is still very often true today.

In 1982, *La Vie en Rose* magazine, in cooperation with the CNTU's status of women committee, conducted a survey of female workers on sexual harassment. Two-thirds of the respondents said they had experienced sexual harassment at work in the form of looks, jokes, words, gestures and physical contact. Bosses, colleagues and clients all engaged in such

---

behaviour. While colleagues were the most frequent perpetrators, the impact on the job was more serious when bosses were the harassers. The women then were faced with a variety of situations including threats of transfer and layoff.

Obviously it was necessary to define sexual harassment. The CNTU's Status of Women Committee proposed the following to the congress of the CNTU in 1984:

Sexual harassment is a sexual comment, a look, repeated and undesired suggestive words, or physical contact which is regarded as objectionable, unpleasant or offensive and is disruptive in the work environment. It can also be defined as pressure for sexual favours when people are at different levels of authority.

Development of Sexual Harassment Policies

At the CNTU, the initial work was the result of a concern related especially to the abuse of authority by superiors with regard to female employees because, of course, working conditions were threatened.

The situations became more complex, however. While the first fears identified were related to harassment by a superior, some client groups served by workers belonging to the CNTU are very vulnerable, for example, in the fields of education and social welfare. In addition, as already mentioned, some client groups represent a higher risk for female workers serving them than others, such as the hotel and restaurant industries. Now we can no longer ignore sexual harassment between peers either.

Some groups are more likely than others to find themselves in situations involving sexual harassment. For this reason, some organizations belonging to the CNTU have shown greater sensitivity to this problem.

In March 1991, the National Federation of Teachers and the Social Affairs Federation, both of which are affiliated with the CNTU, adopted harassment policies that take into account the specific nature of their workplaces. In May 1992, the congress of the CNTU adopted the following recommendation:

> That the CNTU develop a policy to combat sexual
> harassment, including consciousness raising and the
> use of training tools intended for male and female workers.

The central councils in Montreal and Quebec City, which are regional organizations of the CNTU, in turn developed policies on sexual harassment.

Content of Policies: A Procedure for Handling Complaints

With the goal of eliminating all forms of harassment, the sexual harassment policies establish an internal procedure for handling complaints from those who complain of sexual harassment. While they are not identical, the policies do have similarities. For example, a resource person is identified as being responsible for providing the complainant with the necessary support. If the complainant so desires, an effort at mediation with the person accused of harassment will be initiated.

In cases where the complaint is lodged by a child or a mentally disabled person, however, a person with specialized training who is not associated with either party (union or management) could be asked to intervene.

If mediation fails, the complaint is submitted to a committee composed of representatives of various unions or associations involved in the company.

If the committee is unable to resolve the problem, the complaint is forwarded, with the agreement of the complainant, to the human resources unit, *without recommendations*. This unit is then entirely responsible for deciding on disciplinary action.

Representation of Members

If disciplinary action is to be taken, unions must decide on how to represent their members accused of sexual harassment.

To meet the time limits stipulated in the collective agreements, the unions generally file a grievance to contest the disciplinary action while reserving the right to refer it to adjudication.

The policy provides for a thorough investigation, which should enable the union leaders to reach a conclusion on the grievance contesting the disciplinary action. If the complaint proves to be well founded and the disciplinary action is deemed appropriate, the grievance will not be referred to adjudication. If there is any doubt about the truthfulness of the changes or if the disciplinary action is considered too harsh in relation to the offence, the union will refer the grievance to adjudication.

A decision must then be made on the method of defending the person accused of sexual harassment. While the person's right to a thorough defence is to be respected, the complainant's integrity is also to be preserved. This is why the approach at the adjudication hearing will depend on whether the investigation revealed that the disciplinary action was too severe or that the accusations were doubtful or patently false.

Use of Constitutions and By-laws: A Deterrent

Several policies have recommended that unions add a condemnation of any form of sexual harassment to their constitutions and by-laws. Some unions have provided for the expulsion of any member who is found guilty of sexual harassment.

Training: A Necessity

A sexual harassment policy that does not provide for training and awareness-raising measures is generally ineffective.

Responsibility for training is therefore given to the committee that is to apply the policy. Training and awareness raising can take different forms.

The CNTU itself and some of its organizations have developed training sessions for their members in order to prevent sexual harassment. Unions often deal with this matter in their union publications. Others, such as the public sector unions in Quebec, negotiate in order to include policies in the collective agreements.

Conclusion

On a few occasions, the CNTU's Status of Women unit has collaborated with employers by giving training sessions at the workplace. In those cases, however, the employer's request always followed a serious sexual harassment case. Intervention under such conditions is especially difficult because the conflicts have not been resolved, positions have become set, and the work climate has deteriorated badly. In the worst cases, there is almost hostility to any outside intervention.

This is also the case when there has been strong disciplinary action or a sexual harassment adjudication in a workplace: groups form on opposite sides; the climate deteriorates. The victim of sexual harassment who files a complaint is often ostracized by colleagues and sometimes suffers mental problems. In some places, workers still suffer from the ordeal several years later.

For these reasons, the development of a sexual harassment policy in advance appears essential. While it may not succeed in preventing all forms of sexual harassment, which is its main objective, it will at least make the stakes clear and establish a procedure that is known to everyone based on a definition of sexual harassment of which no one will be able to plead ignorance.

Sexual Harassment - Unions at Work

Judy Darcy

Judy Darcy is the National President of the Canadian Union of Public Employees, Canada's largest union. She has been a union activist involved with issues of concern to working women for more than 20 years.

Recently, I was a guest on an Ottawa television phone-in show dealing with women in the workplace. Several women called in to talk about their personal experiences with harassment. They talked about feeling alone in their struggle. They wanted to know about their rights. Some spoke about how they had been forced to quit their jobs because they had reached the point where they just couldn't take it any more.

Besides being victims of this terrible form of workplace discrimination, these women had one other thing in common. None of them belonged to a union. If they had, the odds are that their stories would have been different.

While it is certainly true that sexism has not been stamped out in the unions, it is fair to say that unions have played a key role in the fight against harassment and that more and more unions are taking concrete steps to put an end to this insidious practice.

In CUPE, where more than half of our 412,000 members across Canada are women, we have a particularly strong mandate to act on our policy of zero tolerance of sexual harassment.

We have focused on protecting the victim, while at the same time trying to root out the cause of sexual harassment, namely women's unequal status in the work force and in society. We have also tried to make the links for our members between sexism and harassment and violence against women, and racism, homophobia and discrimination against people with disabilities, so as to show that they are part of the same total picture of injustice.

When CUPE first started dealing with the issue of harassment, we focused our energies on tackling sexual harassment by supervisors and other people with authority in the workplace. But it quickly became apparent that sexual harassment had other manifestations as well, such as harassment between co-workers.

In the latter case, the lines are less clearly drawn than in those involving supervisors. The union is obligated to represent the complainant and the alleged harasser as part of the duty of "fair representation" outlined in federal and most provincial labour legislation. The situation gets even more complicated when you throw in internal workplace politics, friendships and loyalties that can have other workers taking different sides.

It is easy to understand why local union executive members and staff would want their union to develop answers to the important questions raised by this type of harassment. How can the union adequately represent the interests of both parties in a complaint? Are special complaint procedures necessary and, if so, what should they look like? What are the respective roles of the local union, the provincial divisions and the National Union in tackling co-worker harassment?

A couple of years ago, CUPE held a special intensive two-day think-tank to try to come to grips with these issues. As a result of these discussions, we developed for CUPE locals and staff a kit on co-worker harassment. The kit includes background material for collective bargaining, model language for local union bylaws, guidelines for internal complaint procedures, a list of audio-visual resources, an analysis of the union's legal obligation to the complainant and to the alleged harasser, and a sample survey designed to measure the extent of sexual harassment.

The kit outlines several options for dealing with cases of co-worker harassment:

1. Using a "no-discrimination" clause or a specific harassment clause in the collective agreement, the union could file a grievance on behalf of the complainant. If the alleged harasser is found guilty and disciplined, the union may have an obligation to grieve the severity of the disciplinary action.

2. Different staff representatives could be assigned to represent the interests of each party. This is costly in terms of resources, but it seems to achieve the objective of "fair representation."

3. A separate, internal complaint process could be established, perhaps by the bylaws of the local union, so that members could resolve a workplace complaint without involving the employer. However, this approach may be prohibitively expensive for small locals with limited resources, or it may prove to be divisive for the membership. Nor does it acknowledge the legal obligation of the employer to maintain a workplace free from sexual harassment.

The kit stresses that local unions should use these options to design solutions which are appropriate to their particular circumstances.

Some CUPE locals have recently made significant break-throughs in combatting all forms of harassment. CUPE Local 1, representing 1,200 members at Toronto Hydro, negotiated a ground-breaking harassment policy that is an especially significant achievement in a white, male-dominated workplace. The union and management agreed to a joint anti-harassment policy which covers sexual, racial and personal harassment. It recognizes that members have the right to refuse to work when they are being harassed on the job. It clearly outlines management's commitment to maintain a harassment-free workplace and sets out a complaint procedure. This policy does *not* require the complainant to confront the alleged harasser as part of the process, which is a major step forward.

The policy allows workers the right to leave the workplace, with no loss of pay, to file a complaint. It also commits the employer to conduct an immediate investigation of the complaint. The policy is promoted throughout Hydro workplaces with posters and brochures. Local 1 and Toronto Hydro management have also developed jointly a one-day workshop for *all* employees (including management employees) to explain the new policy and complaint procedure.

In Montreal, CUPE Local 301, representing blue collar workers employed by the city, negotiated another significant policy to provide workshops on harassment for its 5,000 members, to be held in the workplace during working hours without loss of pay. The workshops were developed and facilitated by the union. So far, about 2,000 members have participated in these workshops, which confront directly all the myths and stereotypes that cause harassment.

At the national level, we have taken steps to prevent and resolve any incidents of harassment that may occur between union members at union functions. Every two years, delegates from CUPE locals across the country meet for a week to debate issues, establish policies and participate in social events at our national convention. An "Equality Statement" was developed for the 1989 convention which declares:

> As unionists, mutual respect, cooperation and understanding are our goals. We should neither condone nor tolerate behaviour that undermines the dignity or self-esteem of any individual or creates an intimidating, hostile or offensive environment.... Harassment should not be treated as a joke. Harassment focuses on the things that make us different instead of the things that bring us together, like shared concerns about our families, decent wages, safe working conditions, fairness at work and justice in society.

This statement was highlighted in delegates' agenda booklets and was read aloud by the National President as part of the opening ceremonies. It is now standard practice to read the statement at the beginning of other CUPE events like conferences and schools.

At the 1991 national convention, a team of five ombudspersons was put in place to deal with any complaints of racial or sexual harassment. The ombudspersons' team included two union members and three staff, including francophones, racial minorities and women. They were selected for their particular skills and/or experience in dealing with people, and their understanding of the nature of harassment. Prior to the convention, they had all attended a special training session designed to enhance their listening skills and their abilities in problem-solving and conflict-resolution.

Letters were sent to delegates with their pre-convention packages to explain the process. In the convention kits, more than 2,000 delegates received another notice explaining the process and identifying two telephone numbers they could call day or night to register a complaint or get help.

The ombudsperson process was also announced to delegates by the National President at the opening of the convention.

The use of this process was very effective and it generated an enormous amount of discussion among delegates about harassment - what it is, why it is inappropriate behaviour, and why the union should be dealing with it. On the convention floor, many delegates praised the process for promoting discussion, increasing awareness and acting as a deterrent.

At the same convention, the delegates passed an amendment to CUPE's National Constitution expanding the union's objectives to include "the elimination of sexual and racial harassment and harassment based on sexual orientation."

These internal initiatives were pursued not only to develop solutions to a potentially divisive problem, but also to show that solutions *can* be found.

While most of our work has focused on the workplace and in the union, CUPE also recognizes its responsibility to reach out into the community and help to combat that most extreme form of harassment: violence against women. In Toronto, Local 79, our municipal local, has started a housing cooperative which has a clause against domestic violence included in its original bylaws. These bylaws provide that, in the event of abuse, the abuser's lease shall be terminated while the victim may remain in possession. The co-op also provides much needed support and protection for the victim.

Throughout CUPE and throughout the union movement, increasing numbers of union women and union men are standing up and saying "Enough." Violence and harassment, and the sexism, racism and homophobia that underlie them, will no longer be tolerated.

This is an important message to convey, especially in tough economic times when unions are under pressure to give way on the gains they have made on equality issues. CUPE maintains that this is no time to take a step backwards. On the contrary, it is a time for bold initiatives to remedy the social and economic inequality which lies at the root of harassment. It is only by keeping these issues on the front burner and continuing to push for change that the goal of zero tolerance of harassment can one day become a reality.

The Commitment of the FTQ to Eliminate Sexual Harassment

*Clément Godbout and
Lauraine Vaillancourt*

---

*Clément Godbout, General Secretary to the FTQ since
1991, was elected President in December 1993.
Lauraine Vaillancourt is Vice-President of the FTQ
and President of the Status of Women Committee.*

Union Solidarity: An Essential Prerequisite

We at the Fédération des travailleurs et travailleuses du Québec
(FTQ) consider sexual harassment to be a serious problem.
The FTQ is strongly opposed to all manifestations of sexual
harassment, which is an unacceptable form of violence that
compromises the right of women to fair and equitable working
conditions and even their fundamental right to work.

For some 12 years now we have conducted an awareness and
training campaign with our members through our major
networks, including those dealing with the status of women,
education, and health and safety.

We have discussed and debated this matter at conferences and
before parliamentary commissions. During a public consultation
by the provincial Department of Justice in 1981, Claire
Bonenfant, Chairperson of the Conseil du statut de la femme,
reminded those present that "the FTQ spoke out strongly against
sexual harassment in the presentation of its brief before the

commission of the Department of Justice, demanding that the Charter expressly prohibit employer practices involving sexual harassment of female workers." We recommended that it be possible for an employer to be held responsible for harassment, whether these acts are committed by supervisors or by co-workers.

Although we strive for the utmost vigilance with respect to female workers, and although we represent over 150,000 unionized female workers, we must remember that only about 30% of women in Quebec are unionized. However, unionization clearly remains the only real way to defend the rights of workers, regardless of gender, through the creation of work environments based on respect and dignity.

Proposed Means

Sexual harassment can come from line supervisors, co-workers, or clients of the employer, and the consequences are always tragic.

Being a victim of sexual harassment can cause a woman to leave her job, be dismissed or be passed over for a promotion. Harassment creates a climate of tension that can lead to psychological or physical problems for the victim.

Since 1984, there has been a body of case law in Quebec on cases of harassment at work that have been recognized by the Commission de la santé et de la sécurité du travail or that have been recognized with respect to labour relations.

Some collective agreements contain clauses that expressly stipulate the employer's obligation to ensure that the workplace is free from sexual harassment. Moreover, even in the absence of provisions in the collective agreement, the Quebec courts have clearly recognized women's rights to physical and psychological security, whether in the workplace or elsewhere. Let us also remember that section 10.1 of the Quebec Charter of Human Rights and Freedoms stipulates that, in accordance with the right to equal recognition of rights and freedoms, no one may harass a person.

Changing Attitudes: Action Needed to Promote Awareness

Publication of a Guide for Unions: 1982

In 1982, aware of its responsibility in this area, the FTQ published a guide for unions on the prevention and resolution of sexual harassment problems. This guide, still valid today, offers support and advice to women and their unions when faced with this serious problem.

The guide proposes a definition of sexual harassment and discusses its manifestations and effects. It also deals with the many preconceptions surrounding this matter. It analyzes the possible courses of action and remedies available to victims through collective agreements and legislative provisions. Also discussed are investigations and complaint procedures, the promotion of awareness in the workplace, and sources of assistance available.

In light of the success of this guide, which has enabled us to promote awareness among thousands of members, we are preparing a third reprinting.

Specific Training

In addition to having set up specific training for union representatives dealing with the legal basis of sexual harassment protection, which emphasizes unions' responsibilities with respect to labour relations, for some 10 years now we have included a section on sexual harassment in the course on women's living and working conditions. This course has also reached thousands of union activists.

The Example of CUPE

In 1982, one of the unions affiliated with the FTQ, the Canadian Union of Public Employees in Quebec also published a guide for unions on the prevention and resolution of sexual harassment problems in the workplace. This guide has also helped to promote awareness among thousands of members.

Tools for Prevention: Training, Collective Agreements, Constitutions

With its long tradition of training and promotion of awareness, the FTQ has developed not only means of prevention, but also means of resolving harassment problems. Most of the unions affiliated with the FTQ now recognize sexual harassment as a form of discrimination in their collective agreements and, in certain cases, within their constitutions and bylaws. As a result, many agreements contain clauses that allow the two parties to use adjudication and grievance procedures to resolve harassment cases.

At the invitation of the FTQ, many unions have also included, in their constitutions and bylaws, clauses dealing specifically with sexual harassment problems between union members.

Conclusion

Although all of its unions are now taking action on this issue through collective agreements and through courses such as the one on women's living and working conditions, the FTQ has not yet achieved zero tolerance; far from it. Attitudes change very slowly. Our society is experiencing serious economic problems, and there is certainly a connection between poverty and violence.

It is true that we talk more openly about sexual harassment, but we know that this problem is a long way from being eliminated.

Important steps have been taken by unions, and it is unionized female workers who have the best protection. But what about all the rest - the 70 percent of the female labour force made up of women who have little protection and are afraid of losing their jobs? These are women who work part-time or on call, immigrant women, students, and so forth. To all these women, to those who are experiencing this form of violence called sexual harassment, we say, do not remain isolated; talk about it with those around you. We hope that access to unionization will entitle them to the additional protection needed and the support of their fellow workers of either gender. Solidarity remains one of the most effective tools we have.

We will succeed in eliminating sexual harassment when employers truly accept their responsibilities in this area, in particular by adopting policies which establish guidelines to abolish sexism in all its forms. This problem will be completely eliminated when men and women become equals, the power relationship is abandoned, and they can live together in dignity and mutual respect.

Dealing with Sexual Harassment: The Approach of the CAW

Peggy Nash

Peggy Nash *is Director of the Women's and Human Rights programs of the National Automobile, Aerospace and Agricultural Implement Workers Union of Canada (CAW) and Assistant to the President of the union. She is also a Vice-President of the Canadian Labour Congress.*

Many obstacles stand in the way of a woman who wants a "non-traditional" job. They range from a lack of background and training to biased hiring procedures and shift work, to lack of child care facilities and poor transportation. Nevertheless, for decades many women have tried, and some have overcome these barriers and entered the non-traditional industrial work force.

But getting into the work force is only half the battle, for once inside women can still be in for a very rough ride. The messages women get are often hostile, such as: "You are taking away a man's job" or "Since you want to work with men you must either be a lesbian or looking for a man" or "You only got the job because you are a woman, and you can't do the job as well as a man."

These stereotypical messages can translate into forms of behaviour that harass and undermine women at work. They are serious barriers facing all working women, but especially those in non-traditional jobs. They also constitute a real and painful health hazard for women.

As the largest Canadian union in the industrial sector, the CAW (Canadian Auto Workers) has had to take on the issue of harassment in the workplace.

Women in the CAW have complained about workplace harassment for years. If the harasser was a management person, the union had little difficulty in defending the woman. The local union would file a grievance and fight to protect the woman complainant.

But if the harasser was a co-worker, the problem was more complex. How can the union take sides? The union has to defend all members. What power does the union have to make the harasser stop? How can the union go to management to insist on disciplining one of its members? What if the union then has to file a grievance for that member?

It was easier to shrug off harassment as "guys just kidding around" or just part of any industrial work environment. The women would be pressured to have "a sense of humour" and not get everyone upset by pressing a complaint. The easiest solution for the union was to take no action. Women either put up with harassment or quit. Some ended up on sick leave because of stress.

The courageous fight by Bonnie Robichaud in the public sector established the human rights precedent that the employer will be accountable for all workplace harassment, even between co-workers. But a union representative cannot, in all good conscience, tell a member facing co-worker harassment to just complain to the employer. It was clear to us as a union that we had to face our responsibility to act on co-worker harassment.

We consulted widely throughout the union to develop an effective complaint procedure. The CAW Harassment Policy was passed at our 1988 Constitutional Convention.

The CAW policy takes a tough stand on harassment. It makes very clear that harassment is no joke, but rather that it is serious and damaging behaviour. The policy covers racial, sexual, and all other forms of harassment covered by human rights legislation.

Workplaces vary widely, so access to the harassment procedure must be flexible. A person who is being harassed and wants help now can go to any union representative, from a steward to a member of a union committee to the top local leadership. For example, a woman who has been sexually harassed may not want to talk with a male local union president. So she can initiate a complaint with a member of the local union women's committee, human rights committee or employment equity committee.

Once a complaint has been made, the union representative must immediately bring the complaint to the attention of the local union president and the chairperson of the bargaining committee. They must inform the national union of the complaint. They will oversee an investigation, sometimes involving the company. The complaint must be resolved within seven days. Confidentiality is a priority.

When we developed the policy and procedure, we produced eye-catching posters to go up in all workplaces, small booklets outlining the procedure, and a hard-hitting video explaining what constitutes harassment and how the procedure works. These materials were distributed widely throughout the union. We also use local and national union publications, as well as our extensive union education programs, to disseminate information about harassment. We urge locals to get involved and not leave the fight against harassment to those individuals who are being harassed.

Has this policy improved the workplace?

The CAW harassment policy and procedure, along with an effective communications strategy, has helped significantly to educate our members about workplace harassment. The union's clear commitment to confront harassment has prompted many union activists to examine their own behaviour. Broad communication of the policy has sometimes helped prevent behaviour that would constitute harassment. CAW members know that the union's strong stand on harassment means that it will not defend acts of harassment as "harmless fun."

By raising the issue, the policy has encouraged women to come forward and file a complaint, whereas before they might have suffered in silence. Most women just want the harassment to stop. They do not want to draw attention to themselves. They may fear that if the company gets involved the harasser will be disciplined and that perhaps they will face a backlash from other members.

The local union leadership can be very effective in resolving straightforward complaints between two union members. Often a man is unaware of the impact of his actions, and a brief discussion with a union representative can lead to an apology and a change in behaviour. Even where the man knows very well that his behaviour is not acceptable, sometimes it takes another man to take him to task for the behaviour to change. The goal of the procedure is to deal with problems quickly before they escalate. Most complaints are resolved simply, effectively and confidentially.

Where the harasser refuses to apologize or stop the harassment, or where the harassment is more serious or includes physical contact, the union representative usually involves the company. Ultimately, the company is responsible for maintaining a harassment-free workplace. Unfortunately, sometimes it takes the threat of discipline to force a harasser to change. On rare occasions, the harassment is such that the person must be disciplined and perhaps even fired.

Are all harassment complaints dealt with effectively? No, unfortunately not. We still find situations of what I call sexist guerilla warfare: little anonymous acts such as sexist graffiti or pornography strategically placed for a woman to find. There are still the more subtle exclusionary practices and putdowns that are painful to women but that men often fail to notice. Women still face a backlash when they stand up for their rights.

It is essential to have a policy and a procedure, but these alone are not enough. We are increasingly aware of the importance of education on gender, race and disability issues. Our local leadership is responsible for the effective implementation of our harassment policy, but they have not had extensive practical training in resolving harassment complaints. This is now our goal.

We have developed human rights training programs such as a one-week residential human rights course for leadership. We have also negotiated three hours of human rights training for every CAW member at General Motors and some smaller workplaces. In addition, we have developed a week-long program designed specifically for handling harassment complaints.

None of us feels comfortable dealing with harassment. But better training programs can give union representatives the confidence and skills to try and resolve complaints and to intervene in situations before a complaint is necessary. Why should a woman have to complain about pin-ups and face a possible backlash for doing so? It is better for a male union representative to demand that pin-ups be taken down because they are demeaning and against union policy.

These ongoing efforts may seem painstakingly slow for a person facing the agony of harassment on a daily basis. However, step by step, we are making progress. In the CAW we have been conducting a campaign for the last few years to fight male violence against women. Workplace harassment is just one form of this violence. The many leadership debates and education sessions on violence against women are also helping to change the culture within the union and within the workplace.

The CAW, and the broader labour movement, believe that such social change will be very positive. Ultimately the goal is the creation of a more tolerant, respectful egalitarian workplace and society.

Section VI

Bibliography

Selected Bibliography

CANADA

Aggarwal, A.P., *Sexual Harassment: A Guide for Understanding and Prevention*, Toronto, Butterworths, 1992.

Aggarwal, A.P., *Sexual Harassment in the Workplace*, 2nd ed., Toronto, Butterworths, 1992.

Angus Reid Group (The), "Sexual Harassment in the Workplace," *The Reid Report*, Vol. 7, No. 1, 1992, p. 32.

Backhouse, C. and L. Cohen, *The Secret Oppression: Sexual Harassment of Working Women*, Toronto, MacMillan, 1978.

Campbell, D.A., *The Evolution of Sexual Harassment Case Law in Canada*, Kingston, Queen's University, Industrial Relations Centre, 1992.

Canadian Advisory Council on the Status of Women, *CACSW Fact Sheet: Sexual Harassment*, Ottawa, March 1993.

Canadian Human Rights Commission, *Harassment Casebook: Summaries of Selected Harassment Cases*, Ottawa, 1991.

Canadian Human Rights Commission, *What is Harassment?* (pamphlet), Ottawa, 1988 (reprint 1990).

Drapeau, M., *Le harcèlement sexuel au travail: le régime juridique de protection*, Montréal, Editions Yvon Blais, 1991.

Grahame, K., "Sexual Harassment," in C. Guberman and M. Wolfe, eds., *No Safe Place: Violence Against Women and Children*, Toronto, The Women's Press, 1985, p. 121.

Hamilton, J.A., S.W. Alagna, L.S. King and C. Lloyd, "The Emotional Consequences of Gender-Based Abuse in the Workplace," *Women and Therapy*, The Haworth Press, 1987, pp. 155-182.

Labour Canada, Women's Bureau, *Sexual Harassment at Work*, (Fact Sheet), Ottawa, updated 1993.

Labour Canada, Labour Standards, *Sexual Harassment*, (Fact Sheet), Ottawa, 1990.

Labour Canada, *Sexual Harassment in the Workplace*, (Video), Ottawa, 1988.

Larkin, J., "Sexual Harassment: From the Personal to the Political," *Atlantis*, Vol. 17, No. 1 (Fall-Winter), 1991, p. 3-19.

Lowe, G.S., *Women, Paid/Unpaid Work and Stress*, Ottawa, Canadian Advisory Council on the Status of Women, 1989.

Ontario Women's Directorate, *A Time for Action on Sexual Harassment in the Workplace - An Employers Guide*, Toronto, 1993.

Ontario Women's Directorate, *Sexual Harassment in the Workplace*, (Video), Toronto, 1988.

Savoie, D. and V. Larouche, "Le harcèlement sexuel au travail: Définition et mesure du phénomène," *Relations Industrielles*, Vol. 43, No. 3 (1988) pp. 509-30.

Savoie, D. and V. Larouche, "Le harcèlement sexuel au travail: résultats de deux études québécoises," *Relations Industrielles*, Vol. 45, No. 1, (1990).

U.S.A.

Bravo, E. and E. Cassedy, *The 9 to 5 Guide to Combating Sexual Harassment*, New York, John Wiley & Sons, 1992.

Petrocelli, W. & B.K. Repa, *Sexual Harassment on the Job*, Berkeley, Nolo Press, 1992.

DUE